Behind the Scenes at ER

Behind the Scenes at ER

Janine Pourroy

EBURY PRESS
LONDON

First published in the United Kingdom in 1996

1 3 5 7 9 10 8 6 4 2

Copyright © 1995 by Warner Bros.
Cover photograph © 1995 by Warner Bros.
Photo of Michael Crichton, appearing on page 1, copyright ©
1995 by Jonathan Exley.

MRI of brain courtesy of Josh Karpf.
X ray of hand courtesy of Fred Dodnick.

First published in the United States by Ballantine Books, a divi-
sion of Random House, Inc., New York, and simultaneously in
Canada by Random House of Canada Limited, Toronto.

First published in the United Kingdom by Ebury Press
Random House, 20 Vauxhall Bridge Road, London SW1V 2SA

Random House of Australia (Pty) Limited
20 Alfred Street, Milsons Point, Sydney, New South Wales 2061,
Australia

Random House New Zealand Limited
18 Poland Road, Glenfield, Auckland 10, New Zealand

Random House South Africa (Pty) Limited
PO Box 337, Bergvlei, South Africa

Random House UK Limited Reg. No. 954009

Cover design by Jerry Goldie
Interior design by Michaelis/Carpelis Design Assoc., Inc.

Manufactured in the United States of America

A CIP catalogue record for this book is available from the British
Library

ISBN 0 09 181359 X

Contents

Acknowledgments

My initial thanks go to John Wells and *ER*'s talented cast and crew. They made this book possible by taking the time to share their insights and experiences with me, and remained impeccably gracious when things got hectic. Additional thanks to writer Neal Baer, who patiently answered countless medical questions, and to associate producer Wendy Spence for unraveling the mysteries of postproduction.

Gratitude must further be expressed to Cathy Repetti, Fred Dodnick, Nora Reichard, and the other people at Ballantine Books for their commitment to this project—and for making sure things were done right. Thanks also to still photographer Danny Feld, whose visual contributions were invaluable, and to Warner Bros. publicist Nan Sumski for her accessibility and diligent liaison.

Finally, my heartfelt thanks to Fred and Barbara Pourroy, Jessie and Trevor Beld, and my devoted Jim Hatch for working as a team to keep me sane and well loved.

Introduction

There is always, in the beginning, an idea. What becomes the Eiffel Tower or the Declaration of Independence or yesterday's dinner is, at one point, pure thought. A hit movie might start with a lunch shared by two friends and a paper napkin covered with the sudden ink of inspiration. A television sitcom might spring from the memory of striking out on one's own fresh from high school or from fond recollections of long evenings at the neighborhood tavern. What a good idea, a writer might think. Now *this* is a story worth telling.

Getting that story to the screen is an entirely different matter. In the world of television and film the process of transforming an idea into a reality is all too often a painful one. Concepts are mutated, molded, pummeled, and strained through the sieves of "development" until their origins are almost unrecognizable. It is rare indeed when the integrity of the original idea is apparent in its realization.

ER stands as such an exception.

Created by Michael Crichton—author of an impressive list of bestsellers including *Congo*, *Jurassic Park*, *Rising Sun*, and *Disclosure*—*ER* was originally written as a screenplay in 1974 and endured twenty years as a property that nearly everyone agreed was in serious need of repair. With its staccato scenes and frequently jarring portrayal of medicine, Crichton's story about twenty-four hours in a big-city emergency room just didn't make sense in terms of conventional dramatic

ER's creator and executive producer, Michael Crichton.

structure. As far as acceptable formulas went, this one was nowhere near the mark.

Crichton was no stranger to the mercurial world of Hollywood. After having had the majority of his novels translated into motion pictures—and having directed and written the screenplays for *Westworld*, *Coma*, and *The Great Train Robbery*, which was based on his own novel—he was perfectly aware that compromises in structure and content must sometimes be made. *ER* was different. Simply put, it was not a project he was willing to have compromised.

The concept for *ER* emerged from Crichton's years as a student at the Harvard Medical School when he logged innumerable hours in the Massachusetts General Hospital emergency room working toward his degree as a medical doctor. During that time he was also beginning to make his way as a writer and, in fact, paid his way through medical school writing paperback thrillers. Prior to graduation in 1969, he wrote *A Case of Need* and *The Andromeda Strain*. *Five Patients*, a nonfiction work based on his observations and experiences in the emergency room at MGH, was written when he was a fourth-year medical student and published in 1970. Several years later, Crichton turned to the medical world once again, writing his emergency room screenplay, which was originally entitled *EW*—for emergency ward, as they were known at that time.

"I wanted to write something that was based in reality," Crichton recalled. "Something that would have a fast pace and treat medicine in a realistic way. The screenplay was very unusual. It was very focused on the doctors, not the patients—the patients came and went. People yelled paragraphs of drug dosages at each other. It was *very* technical, almost a quasi-documentary. But what interested me was breaking standard dramatic structure. I understood that's what the screenplay did, but I always felt that it was compulsively watchable."

There were times when it seemed hopeful that his screenplay—with its title updated to *ER*—would be produced. But potential buyers always required revisions beforehand: the medical terminology needed to be simplified to levels the audience could easily comprehend; the brief scenes should be extended to more satisfying conclusions; the jumble of story lines was much too confusing to keep track of and needed to be restructured. Crichton was reluctant to do it. "In a certain way, I always felt it was in a special category, a strange thing that was its own with nothing else like it," said Crichton. "Of course, when there isn't anything 'like it,' that's a very difficult animal in the world of entertainment. Everyone wants *Die Hard on a Ship* or some other kind of proven formula translated into a slightly different context. Something that breaks the rules is looked on with suspicion." Although the script was offered to every studio and network over a twenty-year period, the reaction was always the same: the concept was interesting—but it was too technical, too fast paced, too demanding, and too different.

In October 1989, while quietly working on a new novel, Crichton got a phone call from Steven Spielberg. The two had known each other since the early seventies, when one of Spielberg's first official jobs at Universal Studios was to give Crichton a tour of the lot after Crichton had sold *The Andromeda Strain* to Robert Wise. The two men developed a friendship and, years later, when Spielberg mentioned an interest in directing a movie about an emergency room, Crichton told him about *ER*. After some discussion, Spielberg bought the script with the intention of directing it as a feature film.

In the course of their story meetings on the emergency room picture, Spielberg offhandedly asked Crichton what else he was working on. Crichton mentioned a new novel about DNA and dinosaurs. "The minute he said that, my ears shot up," said Spielberg. "I dropped my *ER* notes, sat down next to him, and said, 'So, tell me more.' He rattled off the story and I was absolutely enchanted and mesmerized. I told him I would love to make it as a movie. Michael said, 'Well, I'd love for you to direct it.' So we shook hands and that's the day we made the deal for *Jurassic Park*, well before the book was published."

Discussions about *ER* were temporarily put aside while Crichton completed his work on the novel and Spielberg went on to direct *Hook*. Soon after, Spielberg's attention became focused on filming *Jurassic Park*, which was followed almost immediately by his dedicated commitment to *Schindler's List*. Crichton, in the meantime, became occupied with *Rising Sun* and *Disclosure*. With such distractions, *ER* became the project nobody got around to.

FInally, in October 1993, the time seemed right to discuss once again the making of *ER*—only now the conversation turned to dramatic television. Tony Thomopoulos of Amblin Television had discovered Crichton's screenplay on the back burner at Amblin and suggested that they consider it as a weekly television series instead of a feature. Thomopoulos met with Crichton and John Wells, a writer and producer highly regarded for his work on *China Beach*, to discuss the possibility of producing *ER* as a dramatic serial. Crichton was intrigued by the idea, but remained cautious. He was willing to proceed with *ER* as a series only if it retained the qualities he felt were essential to the project, qualities that had thus far proven impossible for any network to accept.

Although its production now seemed more feasible, Crichton's script

ER's executive producer, John Wells.

continued to cause trepidation in some quarters. With eighty-seven scenes and over a hundred speaking parts, it didn't look like anything anybody had ever seen before. "One of the chief complaints about the script was that you didn't know who you were supposed to care about," said Wells, "that there wasn't a beginning, middle, and end—it was really just a series of small scenes. It had multiple story lines, and many stories that were just one beat and didn't go anywhere else. There was very little standard dramatic through line."

Television, by its very nature episodic, seemed the ideal medium for the unusual format. "*ER* was like a pointillist painting," said Wells. "Looking closely at the bits and pieces of scenes, they seemed not to make sense. But when you stepped back, they added up to an emotional tapestry that was very moving." Painting such a picture in weekly installments would create the kind of impact Crichton had envisioned. The project was presented to Leslie Moonves and Billy Campbell of Warner Bros. Television, who agreed to produce it in association with Crichton's Constant c Productions and Amblin Television, and finally to Warren Littlefield, Don Ohlmeyer, Kevin Reilly, and David Nevins at NBC, who made a serious commitment for a two-hour pilot.

As work began, Crichton and Wells found they were kindred spirits, with a shared vision for the show. "Michael and I had the same ideas about what *ER* should be, what it was going to need to do, and how we'd try to make it into a series," said Wells. "We shared the same concerns about the limitations of most television. Michael felt that there was very little real dramatic writing on television. He felt that people said things to each other they don't really say, that there was a heightened dramatic realism that passes for reality—but that's really not how we communicate. It's particularly not how we communicate in dramatic situations."

At the time, conventional wisdom said that audiences were no longer interested in TV drama. The previous year Wells had pitched five dramatic shows to the networks with disappointing results. Despite his indisputable success with *China Beach*, not a single new drama was picked up. Wells knew that with the involvement of Michael Crichton and Steven Spielberg, *ER* stood a better than average chance of getting on the air. "The big difficulty in dramatic television is to get people to watch it in the first place," he said, "and with the coupling of Steven and Michael, the network had a lot of confidence that they would attract an initial audience. That first viewing is the television equivalent of an opening weekend, and it's very important."

Opening script pages from series premiere, "Day One."

Rev. 07/30/94 (Blue)
Rev. 08/03/94 (Pink)
Rev. 08/08/94 (Yellow)

ER

"Day One"

Written by

John Wells

Directed by

Mimi Leder

Co-Producer
Paul Manning

Produced by
Christopher Chulack

Supervising Producers
Mimi Leder
Robert Nathan
Lydia Woodward

Executive Producers
Michael Crichton
John Wells

A CONSTANT c/AMBLIN PRODUCTION
In Association With
WARNER BROS. TELEVISION
4000 Warner Boulevard
Burbank, California 91522

FIRST DRAFT

July 27, 1994
c 1994
WARNER BROS.
All Rights Reserved

Rev. 7/30/94

ER

"Day One"

ACT ONE

FADE IN:

1   ON DARKNESS   1

The thick, wet, inky blackness of deep sleep. We hear
GENTLE BREATHING. ACROSS the SCREEN slips "ER." It's
gone as quickly as it appeared.

Into this dark dreamworld creeps light. A door opens.

2   EXAM THREE - EARLY MORNING (5:30 AM)   2

                    GOLDMAN
          Susan... Susan...?

A sleeping shape, prone on a gurney, LEWIS. She doesn't
stir. GOLDMAN taps Lewis gently on the shoulder.

                    GOLDMAN
          Susan...?

Lewis stirs, turns to Goldman. Disoriented.

                    GOLDMAN
          You have to get up.

                    LEWIS
              (trying to focus)
          ... What time is it?

                    GOLDMAN
          It's a baby.

                    LEWIS
          A baby?

                    GOLDMAN
          In respiratory arrest...

                                        CUT TO:

3   AMBULANCE ENTRANCE - NIGHT   3

The doors fly open. Two EMT's, CAMACHO and DeBello, leap
out of the rear of an ambulance with a gurney. DeBello
performs CPR, Camacho bags. WRIGHT and Goldman wait.

                                                        2.

4   ER HALLWAY   4

The gurney rounds the corner into the main hall, Lewis
catches up. Camacho runs down the bullet.

                    CAMACHO
          Two-year-old found unresponsive
          in crib. We couldn't get an I.V.

Lewis looks down at the gurney, a small face, an infant.

                    LEWIS
          What'd you find on arrival?

They're rolling down the hallway followed by the nearly
hysterical, half-dressed parents, SHARON and NEVIN
DOWNEY. The gurney hurtles into the ER as our staff
quickly takes over from the EMT's, Lewis in command.

                    CAMACHO
          No spontaneous resps, cyanotic,
          faint pulse at 200. We scooped
          and ran.

The nurses rush for vital signs, tympanic temp, change
over the monitor leads and oxygen. Lewis listens to the
lungs and heart while checking cap refill and questioning
the parents.

                    LEWIS
          What happened?

                    NEVIN
          ... She just stopped breathing...

                    LEWIS
          Has she been sick?
              (Nevin shakes
               'no')
          Any medications, recent trauma?

                    NEVIN
          No. Nothing.

His wife watches in frightened dread. OLIGARIO runs the
accucheck. Lewis listens.

                    LEWIS
          ... Sshhh...!

She grabs the child, holding one arm, the child's head
down, its chest up. Delivers four chest thrusts.

                    SHARON
          ... Oh, my God...

                                        (CONTINUED)

                                                        3.

4   CONTINUED: 4

Lewis flips the baby over, delivers four back blows.
Waits. Nothing. Dammit. Repeats it.

                    LEWIS
          ... Come on...
              (off nothing)
          Laryngoscope.

Wright has the intubation tray. Lewis works the laryngoscope into the baby's throat.

                    LEWIS
          Magill forceps.

Lewis fishes in the baby's throat.

                    LEWIS
          ... Where are you...?

It's very quiet. Tense. Everyone watches Lewis. It
takes an eternity. Slowly, carefully, she extracts the
tweezers. And with them -- an earring. An audible GASP
comes from the CHILD. But it isn't over.

                    LEWIS
          3.5 E.T. tube.

Lewis works in the tube, tapes it, hooks it to the bag.

                    LEWIS
          Hyperventilate her. Blood sugar?

                    OLIGARIO
          Twenty.

                    LEWIS
          Give me a 14 gauge. I'll go in
          interosseus.

                    SHARON
          ... Is she gonna be alright now?
              (to the EMT's)
          Is she gonna be okay?

They don't answer. The lack of an answer is the answer.
Lewis stares at the monitor. Wishing. Hoping. Praying.
Nothing. Nothing. God, will anything ever happen?

Then... a movement. Upwards. The BABY moves slightly.
TAKES A BREATH, CRIES. Goldman smiles.

                    SHARON
          Oh, my God... Oh, my God...

                                        (CONTINUED)

With Crichton and Wells serving as executive producers and the project propelled by Steven Spielberg and the phenomenal success of *Jurassic Park*, *ER* finally became a reality. The pilot was aired on Monday, September 19, 1994. Three days later, on September 22, the series premiere—entitled "Day One"—was broadcast at ten P.M. in the Thursday night time slot it would claim as its own.

Crichton had always maintained that it was fundamental for the series to deviate from established dramatic television traditions and maintain a strong sense of realism—and he remained convinced that audiences would respond positively to that kind of truthful storytelling. "Television over many years has drifted into something like kabuki," he noted, "a highly stylized representation, a theatricality that doesn't really relate to people's lives anymore. The audience looks at it because that's what is on, but most dramas have lost what television originally had—a real contact with the outer world. I think *ER* showed that you could reestablish that contact."

Chapter 1
The Pilot

The screen is black and we hear the faint sound of what seems to be snoring. A white rectangle of light suddenly silhouettes the form of a woman who has just opened a door. A man is revealed, dressed in medical scrubs and lying on a gurney. It is Dr. Mark Greene, dead asleep at five A.M., being awakened to care for his first patient of the day. The patient turns out to be his friend and coworker, Dr. Doug Ross, who has just reeled into the hospital, quite drunk, and is in immediate need of chemically induced sobering. Greene reluctantly gets up. It is another long and very full day in the ER.

For the next two hours, the audience is offered "an account of 24 hours in a Chicago hospital emergency ward on March 17, St. Patrick's Day"—as noted by Michael Crichton at the beginning of his script for the pilot. The day includes a scaffolding that collapses, injuring twelve; an eight-year-old with a bleeding ulcer; a thirteen-year-old with an ectopic pregnancy; a nurse who has taken an overdose of drugs; and more than a dozen other major and minor crises. In between these emergencies fall the everyday routines of filling out paperwork and having lunch with a spouse. Chaos is juxtaposed with calm; sunshine gives way to snowfall, which gives way to rain, and lengthy scenes keep tempo alongside the merest glimpses of plot and character.

And it is only the beginning.

To adapt Crichton's original screenplay for the pilot required little alteration. A few scenes were adjusted to reflect medical advances and give minor hints of story lines to pique audience interest in some of the characters. "With a two-hour feature, the audience doesn't need to come back and see it next week," said John Wells. "They just need to be informed and interested for the two hours they've already invested. A pilot is different. A pilot needs to have plot points that remain open-ended so people want to know what's going to happen next. With *ER* it was a matter of taking something that was a closed system and opening it up a bit. It was a very subtle thing."

The next step was to assemble the production personnel to film the pilot. Veteran television director Rod Holcomb was hired to work with Wells and Crichton in leading the project. Having directed the pilots for *The Greatest American Hero, The A-Team, Wiseguy, The Equalizer*, and *China Beach*, among others, Holcomb came to *ER* with a good understanding of uncommon television formats. He had also experienced remarkable success. Of the thirteen pilots he had directed at that point, eleven had been sold to the networks.

Like Wells, Holcomb was immediately compelled by Crichton's screenplay. "I remember calling John Wells after I'd read the script and saying, 'I'm exhausted,'" he recalled. "It was one hundred fifty-seven pages long, which was about forty pages longer than a typical pilot script, and it took a tremendous amount of attention to read. But I found it quite interesting. I thought there were some wonderful characters in it. There was a lot of medical verbiage along with the storytelling, but as I read it more closely—and had discussions with John and Michael—it became clear that the verbiage was only like a gurney wheel turning. It actually served to motivate the patients and the doctors surrounding them."

For Holcomb, much of *ER*'s appeal was derived from the way the characters were revealed. "In years past, when it came to dramas, the storytelling tended to be very pedantic. The story needed to have such exacting explanations made in order to make it credible that oftentimes the audience lost the ability to see the main characters. With *ER* it was apparent that the characters were revealed through the fragmented narrative."

Along with Holcomb, a first-rate production team was gathered to shoot the pilot for NBC. Dennis Murphy signed on as producer, Thomas Del Ruth joined the company as director of photography, and production designer Michael Helmy was hired to create realistic emergency room sets on location at Linda Vista Hospital in Boyle Heights, an abandoned hospital in the Los Angeles area frequently used in television and film production.

Wells and Holcomb at once began casting the actors who would bring Crichton's characters to life. Finding the right ensemble was crucial: the individuals they hired would be responsible for originating the roles, as well as potentially carrying them through a five-year run should the pilot be picked up as a series. "Under ordinary circumstances," said Wells, "there is a certain amount of pressure to use recognizable names or faces when casting shows. The networks provide extensive lists of suggested performers to choose from—not for any cynical reason, just for the obvious business reason that nobody's going to watch your show unless they know somebody to watch it for. *ER* was different. We felt so confident that people would watch the show because of Michael Crichton's and Steven Spielberg's involvement that we were able to start casting the show without any of the usual pressures. We had the freedom to cast the best actors for the parts. When the word got around that we were going to do a serious drama—and that Michael and Steven were involved—we heard from literally thousands of people who wanted to be on the show."

The casting process begins with a final script and well-defined characters. The casting director then sends a "breakdown" (a description of the characters complete with production details) to agents and managers. Several days later, the casting director begins to receive photos and résumés suggesting possible actors for the parts.

While this kind of information is useful, the casting director's personal knowledge of an actor is even more significant. For example, an actor may have turned in a remarkable performance on another show or given a particularly memorable audition for something completely unrelated. Occasionally other casting directors offer suggestions. Using all possible resources, the casting director then compiles a list of potential actors for a part, after which auditions and callbacks are held.

George Clooney as Dr. Doug Ross.

After narrowing the list to several possibilities, the casting director then arranges auditions for the producers and director. If an actor makes it over that hurdle, he or she must still be approved by the network before receiving the role. For the pilot, this arduous process was skillfully managed by head of Warner Bros. casting Barbara Miller and casting director John Levey.

The role of Dr. Doug Ross was the first to be assigned, and resulted from a much more straightforward approach than the usual process of auditions and callbacks. In fact, within two days after the pilot received a green light, George Clooney was hired as *ER*'s charming but dissolute pediatric resident. His recent work on *Sisters* had earned him considerable popularity as a leading man and, as a contract player at Warner Bros., he immediately came to mind as soon as Miller and Levey saw the pilot script. "George Clooney and the Doug Ross character seemed like a complete fit," said

Levey. "If you're going to cast a character with behavior that people don't approve of—such as drinking too much and cheating on his girl-friend—you need someone who balances that behavior with their innate charm and attractiveness. George is one of those people who can get away with pretty much anything because he's adorable."

Clooney's enthusiasm for the role, along with an impressive audition, struck a chord with John Wells and Rod Holcomb. "As soon as the show got a pickup, George called me and said, 'Doug Ross is my part,'" Wells recalled. "I hadn't even hired a director at that point. But as soon as I hired Rod—which happened to be on a Thursday—George called me again, and on Friday he came in to read for the show. He had memo-rized an entire scene from the pilot—the one where his character has a confrontation with the attorney who's abusing her child. He was terrific. Rod gave him a couple of adjustments, which he did beautifully, and when he walked out of the room I said, 'Boy, he's great.' We hired him right away."

The next role to be assigned was that of Dr. Mark Greene, a talented and emotionally stable fourth-year resident whose personal life is slow-ly being pulled apart by the strains of a difficult marriage. The part went to Anthony Edwards, whose work in such varied productions as *Top Gun*, *The Client*, and *Northern Exposure* had long captured Wells's interest. "After we got George, the pieces began to fall into place," said Levey, "and the constraints and necessities for the Dr. Greene part changed. I made a list of fifteen or twenty possible actors for the part and Anthony Edwards's name appeared on it. John Wells immediately thought Anthony would be great. So we brought him in dur-ing the first casting session and everybody felt he was the perfect balance to George—we had an immoral center in George and a moral center in Anthony."

Wells had known Anthony Edwards on and off profes-sionally for quite a while. "I wanted to cast Anthony right away," said Wells, "but we got word from his agent that he was going to be unavailable to shoot the pilot because a small movie that he was supposed to direct had just got-ten financed. I was very disappointed. We saw other actors for another month and a half and never saw any-body else who was as right for the part. So I started hav-ing John Levey call Anthony's agent to see if we could work something out. It just didn't seem possible. Finally, we got a phone call saying that the movie had been delayed for a week, which gave Anthony the time to do the pilot—but it was only a twenty-four-hour notice,

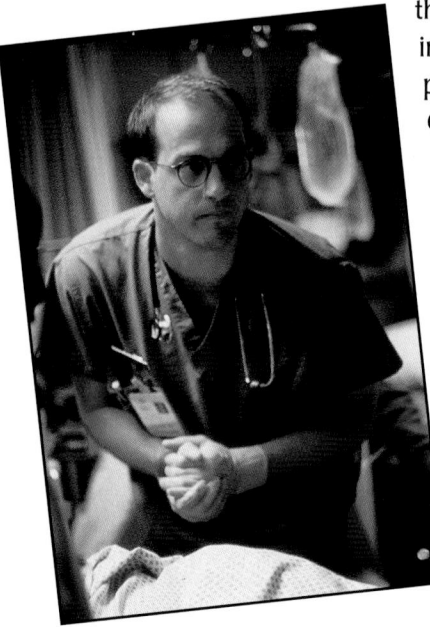

Anthony Edwards as Dr. Mark Greene.

Sherry Stringfield as Dr. Susan Lewis.

and he still had to read for the network. He came in and did the single most extraordinary reading I'd seen. Those pilot auditions are very tough—you come into a room and there are about twenty-four people watching you. The pressure is extraordinary because if the series goes, it's a make-it-or-break-it thing for an actor. Anthony came in under those circumstances and did a beautiful reading." NBC signed off on Edwards without hesitation. The movie company rescheduled the production of his film, and Edwards was able to begin directing immediately after finishing the pilot for *ER*.

The next character to fall into place during the casting process was Dr. Susan Lewis, a hardworking second-year resident struggling to find self-confidence in a demanding and highly competitive profession. The part went to Sherry Stringfield, who had recently appeared as a lawyer who was also the ex-wife of David Caruso's Detective John Kelly on *NYPD Blue.* "John Wells and I were working on a project about a sports bar several seasons before *ER*," said Levey, "when we fell in love with Sherry. We felt she had that special combination of groundedness and maturity—and also a silly side, which hadn't been revealed. When it came time to cast *ER* she unfortunately was already committed to *NYPD Blue.*" Although it seemed clear that Stringfield was out of the running for *ER*, Wells and Levey continued to follow her career.

Wells recalled, "When *ER* got picked up, her agent called me and said that he didn't think her part on *NYPD Blue* was going to continue. The show had really become about the men, and the women were being used very infrequently." Wells and Holcomb were open to considering Stringfield for the part, but there remained one significant hitch: she was still under contract to Steven Bochco Productions. "Sherry came in and read for us in my office, and we worked on the script for a couple of hours. She was great and we really wanted to use her, but we had to wait and see whether Steven was going to let her go. Ultimately he did, and was very gracious about it."

The fourth piece of the ensemble puzzle was third-year medical student John Carter, a young man whose limited experience leaves him completely unprepared for the frenetic pace of the ER. "The part of John Carter was very difficult to cast because it required the ability to do physical comedy," said

Noah Wyle as John Carter.

Levey. "Yet it was also important that the character didn't look like an idiot. The other side, the vulnerability and intelligence, were every bit as important as comedic ability."

Noah Wyle, who had appeared in *A Few Good Men* and *Swing Kids*, was among several very talented actors to compete for the part. "Other people who tried out for the part were revealed as doing one dimension of the character," said Levey. "But every time Noah read we saw a new dimension; he found something else. By the time he read the scene where his character has almost thrown up during a trauma scene and Dr. Greene talks to him outside, telling him not to change, we knew we had found our Carter. Noah didn't have much dialogue in that scene, but that was it. We knew that if he could be funny and empathetic *and* play a believable doctor that we had all three sides of the character."

Even more difficult to cast was the part of Carter's supervisor, Dr. Peter Benton, a tough-minded second-year surgical resident with an attitude. "We had auditioned and talked about some of the most fabulous African American talent in the city for the part of Benton," said Levey. "And we were all over the place—from a guy in his early forties to a guy in his early-to-mid-twenties, from someone much younger than Anthony Edwards to someone much older than Anthony Edwards. But we felt that Dr. Benton really needed to be a contemporary of the oldest guy on the show, neither younger nor older. And we simply couldn't find the right actor for the part."

It wasn't until they were ready to begin filming that Wells and Holcomb finally gained access to Eriq La Salle, who had been shooting

Eriq La Salle as Dr. Peter Benton.

another pilot for Warner Bros. called *Under Suspicion in Portland*. "We actually rearranged the shooting schedule so that the Benton character wouldn't start right away," said Wells. "Even so, we still had only four days we could shoot without him. Eriq walked into the office on a Tuesday—the day we started shooting. We took him to the network on Wednesday, and he started the following day."

The first scene La Salle was required to shoot was the four-page "walk and talk" with Noah Wyle, where Benton shows his charge around the emergency room spouting pages of medical jargon. "Eriq really jumped into the deep end," said Wells. "He did a *very* difficult scene and he did it in twenty-four takes. It was filmed as one continuous piece without any edits. It turned out to be one of the great moments in the pilot."

Although the part of emergency room head nurse Carol Hathaway was cast well before the pilot began filming, Julianna Margulies was less certain of a continuing role. After all, her character attempts suicide within the context of the story. "Hathaway was supposed to die in the pilot," said Wells, "and we really agonized about it, because it seemed very much a television convention to have her *not* die. In serious television, however, when you have a wonderful actress who delivers great material for you, you swallow hard and get over the story problems. In the pilot, she is medically dead; everything that is said about her points in that direction. But Julianna was so wonderful that Michael Crichton and I said, okay, we'll strain the plausibility in this case and keep Hathaway alive and just have her recover fast. Julianna's a wonderful actress and we were really very lucky to get her."

"Ensemble casting is particularly difficult because you really have to balance it out," Barbara Miller observed. "It's not as if you find one person for the lead and then assign the rest of the parts; the parts for *ER* were pretty equal all the way around." In addition to determining the principal players, Miller and Levey were responsible for casting nearly *ninety* additional speaking parts—a number significantly greater than the maximum fifty typically used in two-hour pilots.

Julianna Margulies as Nurse Carol Hathaway.

Rod Holcomb approached the pilot for *ER* with the same philosophy he always does—as if it were a feature film, complete and whole unto itself. He advised his cast to do the same. "I always tell my actors to think of the pilot as a movie, to completely dispense with any thought of being on the air for five years. I tell them that the only thing that matters is playing a part in this two-hour feature—and it may be the last time they play that part, so they'd better do a good job. That's the only philosophy for doing pilots. Only then are they free to say, 'I'm not worried if this doesn't go on. I'm only worried about the work that is presently at hand.' I don't know if it's liberating for the actors to hear or not, but I keep saying it. The truth is, I keep saying it to myself."

Both interiors and exteriors for the pilot were filmed at the Linda Vista Hospital location during a brisk twenty-one-day shoot beginning in mid-March 1994. The hospital interiors were refurbished with windowed walls and lots of open areas to allow for a multilayered visual impact. The floors and walls were covered with the same precisely patterned tiles and linoleums that carried over to the weekly series.

While filming the pilot, Holcomb, working with Wells and Crichton,

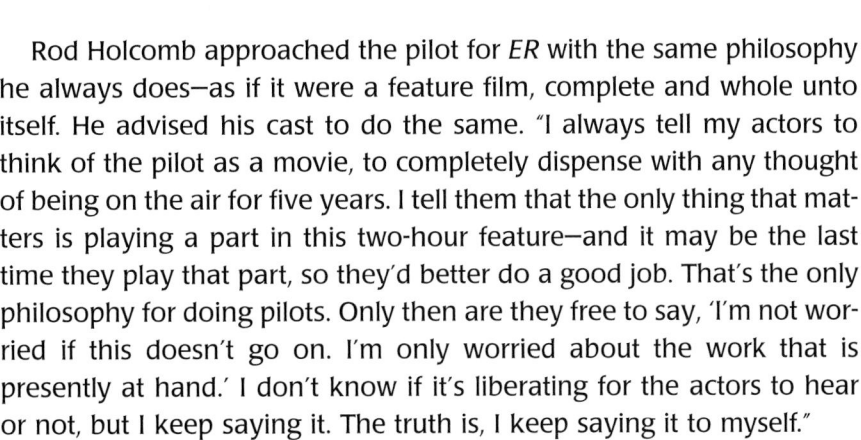

paid strict attention to pace, visual style, and establishing the technical dialogue that propelled the drama. "It was hard for the actors to say these things at first," Crichton recalled. "It was a big mouthful. And early on, they needed to learn how to take over the situation like real doctors, which meant that if they were interested in the patient's abdomen, they didn't look at a patient's face—which goes against the actor's instinct. And sometimes the actors would look to the patient for approval, which is something a real doctor wouldn't do. The actors had to learn how to take charge, and not want the patients to like them. They all got very good at that."

After long hours of rehearsal and multiple takes per scene, the director and producers had gathered the footage they were after. Working with editor Randy Jon Morgan, they pieced together an intricate story with cohesion and style—and established the powerful emotional impact Crichton had originally envisioned in his script.

Once the final postproduction elements of sound editing, sound effects, and music (composed by James Newton Howard) were satisfactorily mixed in with the footage, both Warner Bros. and NBC showed the pilot to focus groups across the country. This was followed by a process of note taking and discussion based on audience feedback. An electronic tally was derived from this information and indicated a score so high that it was difficult to ignore. *ER* received the highest test scores of any dramatic pilot in recent history.

"The pilot was about a day in an emergency room," said Holcomb. "It was very plain and simple. It defined premises, it defined parameters, and it defined how people had to exist within that framework. People came and went, and not all the stories were finished, because in real life, you're not always going to be there to see how something finishes up. But we gave the audience a taste of something real. That was the mission, and I think we accomplished it."

FIRST SEASON EPISODES

Pilot
Written by Michael Crichton
Directed by Rod Holcomb

Episode 1
"Day One"
Written by John Wells
Directed by Mimi Leder

Episode 2
"Going Home"
Written by Lydia Woodward
Directed by Mark Tinker

Episode 3
"Into That Good Night"
Written by Robert Nathan
Directed by Charles Haid

Episode 4
"Hit and Run"
Written by Paul Manning
Directed by Mimi Leder

Episode 5
"Chicago Heat"
Story by Neal Baer
Teleplay by John Wells
Directed by Elodie Keene

Episode 6
"Another Perfect Day"
Story by Lance Gentile
Teleplay by Lydia Woodward
Directed by Vern Gillum

Episode 7
"9 ½ Hours"
Written by Robert Nathan
Directed by James Hayman

Episode 8
"ER Confidential"
Written by Paul Manning
Directed by Daniel Sackheim

Episode 9
"Blizzard"
Story by Neal Baer and Paul Manning
Written by Lance Gentile
Directed by Mimi Leder

Director Felix Alcalà (seated center).

Episode 10
"The Gift"
Written by Neal Baer
Directed by Felix Alcalà

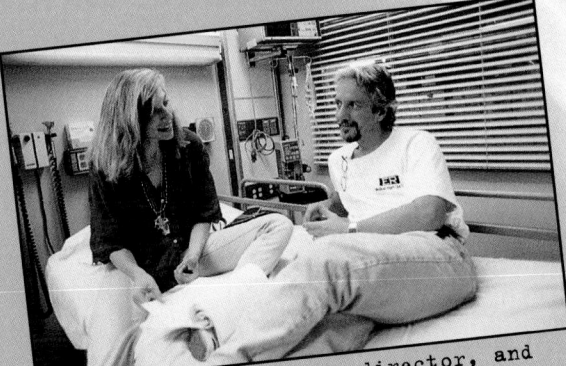
Leslie Glatter, episode director, and Dr. Lance Gentile, medical consultant and writer.

Producer Christopher Chulack, executive producer John Wells, co-executive producer and director Mimi Leder.

Episode 11
"Happy New Year"
Written by Lydia Woodward
Directed by Charles Haid

Episode 12
"Luck of the Draw"
Written by Paul Manning
Directed by Rod Holcomb

Episode 13
"Long Day's Journey"
Written by Robert Nathan
Directed by Anita Addison

Episode 14
"Feb. 5, '95"
Written by John Wells
Directed by James Hayman

Episode 15
"Make of Two Hearts"
Written by Lydia Woodward
Directed by Mimi Leder

Episode 16
"The Birthday Party"
Written by John Wells
Directed by Elodie Keene

Episode 17
"Sleepless in Chicago"
Written by Paul Manning
Directed by Christopher Chulack

Episode 18
"Love's Labor Lost"
Written by Lance Gentile
Directed by Mimi Leder

Episode 19
"Full Moon, Saturday Night"
Written by Neal Baer
Directed by Donna Deitch

Episode 20
"House of Cards"
Written by Tracey Stern
Directed by Fred Gerber

Episode 21
"Men Plan, God Laughs"
Written by Robert Nathan
Directed by Christopher Chulack

Episode 22
"Love Among the Ruins"
Written by Paul Manning
Directed by Fred Gerber

Episode 23
"Motherhood"
Written by Lydia Woodward
Directed by Quentin Tarantino

Episode 24
"Everything Old Is New Again"
Written by John Wells
Directed by Mimi Leder

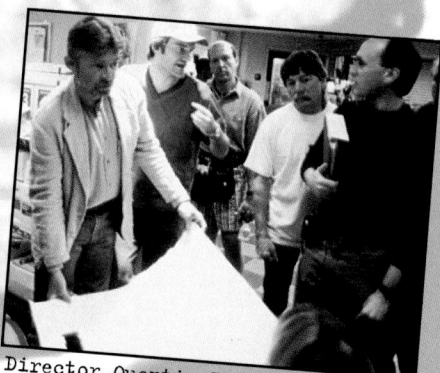

Director Quentin Tarantino (with hat).

Chapter 2
Writing and Research

Television is a medium of shadow and light.

The flickering characters we watch from our living room sofas are not really playing out scenes from their lives; they are actors speaking lines they have memorized from a script someone else has written. They do not exist in any real place; they perform on sets made of breakaway walls and borrowed coffee tables. All too often, even the laughter is contrived.

There are, however, moments when truth filters through these illusory images. As an audience, we know the difference. We can tell when characters make connections, and when they miss. We *know* that life is flawed and messy and imprecise and fabulous—and it does us good when we see that reflected in the shows we watch. While being entertained, we discover that we are not alone, and television becomes what good theater has always been: a transcendent experience.

On *ER*, the reality is added in layers that begin with the writing. Characters are revealed in glimpses, not in heavy-handed declarations. As doctors they are heroes, but we discover behind their boldness, fragility. And humanity. Truth slips through the drama with such subtlety that it leaves us thinking about it the next day at work.

Michael Crichton established this reality in the pilot, but in continuing the show as a weekly series, the producers faced daunting challenges. Crichton recalled, "None of us was entirely sure how to make the series work. John's feeling was, 'We know the elements, we'll have to play with them and see what happens.' But the fragmentary storytelling techniques established in the pilot—the idea that you only saw intermittent glimpses of ongoing events and characters—were difficult to use on a weekly basis. Because there couldn't be a formula. There could be no obvious rules that tied the incidents in an episode together because if there were, the audience would quickly sense that and the show would lose its realism. No one had ever attempted a TV show like this, and there was a real possibility that it just couldn't be done. But *ER*'s writers do it, week after week. Breathtakingly well."

It was also important to retain the medical sensibilities Crichton had insisted on for so many years. "One of the things we decided early on," said John Wells, "was not to pander to the viewer medically. Traditionally, medical shows have had the attitude that the viewer has to understand what's going on medically at all times. So you hear characters saying a lot of ridiculous things like 'It's time to do the laparotomy! Joe, get that tube so we can see if there's blood in his stomach!'—when, clearly, everybody in the scene would know what a laparotomy was. Instead, we allowed the audience to feel as if they'd stepped into a real hospital, and decided not to underestimate their intelligence. We knew it wasn't necessary for them to understand all the medicine to follow the story. It's sort of like watching a conversation in a foreign language. You depend on your other senses. You watch the body language between the characters. You see the gestures, you listen to the tone of voice, and you very clearly see what's going on. I think that takes you deeper into the drama of the scene, because you're not worried about the specifics medically, which aren't all that important, anyway. You get a sense of what's happening and what the stakes are for everyone involved."

Producer Paul Manning.

Medical consultant Dr. Lance Gentile.

Co-executive producer Lydia Woodward.

Additionally, the producers felt it was essential to keep the focus on the doctors, not the patients. "Generally speaking, doctors in medical shows have been nice, earnest people who are very talented," said Wells. "They're either the Ben Casey kind of gruff or the Marcus Welby kind of warm and empathetic—and they stay with the patient throughout the course of an hour-long episode. But in reality, doctors' lives are not much like that. I've had a lot of doctors tell me, 'I can stand here and hold the patient's hand, or I can go help two or three other people.' In an emergency room setting, that's particularly true. The extra time a doctor spends with one person is time taken away from somebody else. Because we wanted to stay realistic in that way, we needed to focus on the emotional journey of the doctor, unlike the traditional medical story, which tended to focus on the emotional journey of the patient."

Such journeys begin with well-considered scripts, determined in part at lengthy writers meetings where Wells and the other writer/producers lay out the show's intricate multiple story lines. Working with Wells are co-executive producer Lydia Woodward; co-executive producer Carol Flint, who joined the production team the second season; coproducer Paul Manning; medical consultants Dr. Lance Gentile and fourth-year Harvard medical student Neal Baer; and staff writer Tracey Stern. (Robert Nathan, one of *ER*'s original writer/producers, left the show after the first season to produce *The Client*.) In-house director Mimi Leder is also involved in the story process, as are Michael Crichton and Steven Spielberg, who regularly offer their ideas as well.

Plot issues are discussed, character motivation and growth are examined, and slowly, the writers begin to determine the specifics for each episode—and the overlapping, intertwining stories that will eventually make up a season's worth of episodes.

Until the early eighties, dramatic shows tended to have one basic story line per show. Series such as *Mannix* or *The Defenders*, for example, dealt with solving a single case within the confines of their allotted hour. That style of dramatic television changed in 1981 with the advent of Steven Bochco's *Hill Street Blues*, when a kind of Dickensian multiple story line was introduced. This style of storytelling was typically told using three or four different stories—an A, a B, and a C story, with a D story, or "comic runner"—woven together throughout the course of the program.

With *ER*, the producers decided to reinvent dramatic television once again. "We usually have anywhere from nine to eighteen stories running in any episode," said Wells. "We wanted the pace to move in a way that would hold the audience's interest. The joke around here was that

ER is the show for the era of remote controls because there is no need to channel surf: all you have to do is hang around for a minute or two and you're going to see another story. People have called to tell us that they thought the show was only a half hour long because there was so much in it. It literally moved so fast that they weren't able to gauge the length compared to a normal hour of dramatic television. Well, even though those elements had worked in the pilot, there was still some concern about bringing them to the series. We had a lot of people warning us, 'The audience may enjoy going to see the movie *Speed*, but they don't want to see it every night.' To which I was always thinking, 'Why not?'"

With that philosophy in mind, the producers steadfastly refused to change *ER*'s pace. Within the reality of the emergency room setting, it made sense for the medical stories to happen quickly and be resolved within a few scenes—after all, a real ER is not designed to handle long-term patient care. Just as realistically, it made sense for the character arcs—or personal journeys—to take place over longer periods of time.

"We didn't do a single episode about Benton's mother's death," said Wells. "Benton's mother's death takes eleven episodes, because that's the way these things really happen. They're painful and slow and one day's good and one day's bad, and those things in our lives take a very long time. We didn't do an episode about Greene's marriage falling apart, because marriages don't fall apart in a day. Greene's marriage falling apart may take two or three years. We use the reality of the medicine to carry through to the reality of the personal stories. We follow the characters as they live their lives in *real* time, and I think that heightens the sense of realism on the show."

The balance was clearly effective. The public response to *ER* was immediate and overwhelming, and eventually NBC ordered twenty-four episodes the first season, two more than the usual twenty-two for dramatic television.

ER's writers work initially as a group, and begin by planning the character arcs that will take place over several episodes. Personal stories are developed before medical elements are introduced into the scripting process. Weeks of painstaking discussion and revision must pass before acceptable plots have been established for each episode. "You're always looking for a way into a character," Lydia Woodward observed. "And the only way for an audience into a character is through behavior. It's a discovery process, which is actually what makes writing fun, because you don't know everything going in. A lot of it is the chemistry between the actors, and between the writers and actors. Sometimes you can see where a certain scene will work particularly well for a certain character.

That's good, because on a show like this—with so many elements running throughout each episode—you're constantly mixing it up."

These human revelations add another layer of realism to the storytelling. "The secret to *ER* is that the characters are not overwritten," Steven Spielberg noted. "The audience has learned who the characters are the way people make friends with each other. A friendship evolves out of understanding who the other person is over a period of time, not overnight. So audiences who watch *ER* learn about the characters the way they would make a friend, slowly and with a great deal of respect and admiration."

Once the character arcs have been determined, the writers turn to the medical stories that take place in the emergency room. All medical "beats" originate from real-life episodes gathered by Tracey Stern, Neal Baer, and Lance Gentile, who have developed an extensive web of contacts—numbering in the hundreds—from coast to coast. Emergency room nurses and physicians regularly share their experiences with the *ER* researchers via telephone. The writers also log numerous hours at local trauma centers, including County USC, UCLA, and White Memorial Hospital. Additionally, Stern conducts an annual "Nurse's Night" at Warner Bros., where local emergency room nurses gather to share their professional and personal experiences. All together, these medical anecdotes fill an enormous three-ring reference binder divided into three different categories: serious, humorous, and workplace.

"Nurses have a good ability to relay the human interest side of what goes on in an ER," said Stern. "Doctors have a tendency to be a little clinical and are generally harder to get in touch with. People send me the names of nurses who are interested in sharing their 'war stories,' as we call them. Workplace stories will be different in a teaching hospital than at a private hospital, but I'm not picky—I'll take stories from anywhere. And I hear everything. I want to know about what they do for fun with the other nurses and with doctors. I want to hear about the strange patients, the strange cases. It's very, very interesting. The Emergency Nurses Association has been wonderful in helping out. I have also been to the Emergency Nurses Conference in San Antonio. I've talked with literally thousands of nurses."

Many of the medical stories come directly from Neal Baer, who, as a third- and fourth-year Harvard medical student doing rotations at UCLA, Cedars-Sinai, and Massachusetts General, has firsthand familiarity within a current emergency room setting. Baer contributes to the research process, but serves more often as resident storyteller. "Many of the medical stories come from my experience as a medical student, when I spent a lot of time in the ER," he said. "For example, I had a

Real-life surgical EMT and ER extra Risa Stefani.

Real-life physician's assistant student and ER extra Malette LeBlanc in a scene with Yvette Freeman.

patient with HIV who had the hiccups, and another patient with Alzheimer's disease who sang opera. Both of these cases ended up on *ER*. Some things are so strange that you wonder if they could really happen, but every story we've told is based on a real experience. We're just careful to change them enough so they're not identifiable with anybody."

For the second season, Baer complied a comprehensive section for the *ER* medical reference book called "Fourth-Year Medical Student," which includes general information about the personal, social, academic, and political issues of being a medical student. This information is most useful in scripting character arcs for John Carter, but it also provides a wealth of real-life trivia for the writers to use in coloring the medical milieu. "I think the audience can judge when something is not real," Baer said, "and that breaks the flow of the experience. If someone who is watching the show says, 'Oh, could that *really* happen?' that means they're losing the thread of the drama."

Baer serves as a sounding board for story ideas. "I spend a lot of time just hashing things out with the other writers. For instance, Paul Manning came to me during the first season and told me, 'I want to do something where Wild Willy [Michael Ironside] and Greene are not getting along and have there be some kind of trauma where they can disagree.' And I said, 'Well, you can have an emergency where one thinks that you should intubate, and one thinks you shouldn't.' Their argument over the procedure turned up in Episode 22, 'Love Among the Ruins.' "

Lance Gentile contributes to the show in a similar manner. A career ER physician, Gentile's interest in film drew him to USC Film School, from which he graduated in 1990. He also cowrote and associate produced an HBO film called *State of Emergency*. With this diverse background, Gentile offers insights from both a medical and a cinematic perspective.

Gentile works with the scripts, the ideas, and the stories that go into every episode, literally following a script from preproduction through postproduction. For example, when a writer is considering a certain illness or injury as one of the medical beats for a script, Gentile—along with Baer and on-set technical adviser Dr. Joe Sachs—is consulted as to the specifics of the proposed case. A treatment plan is written and

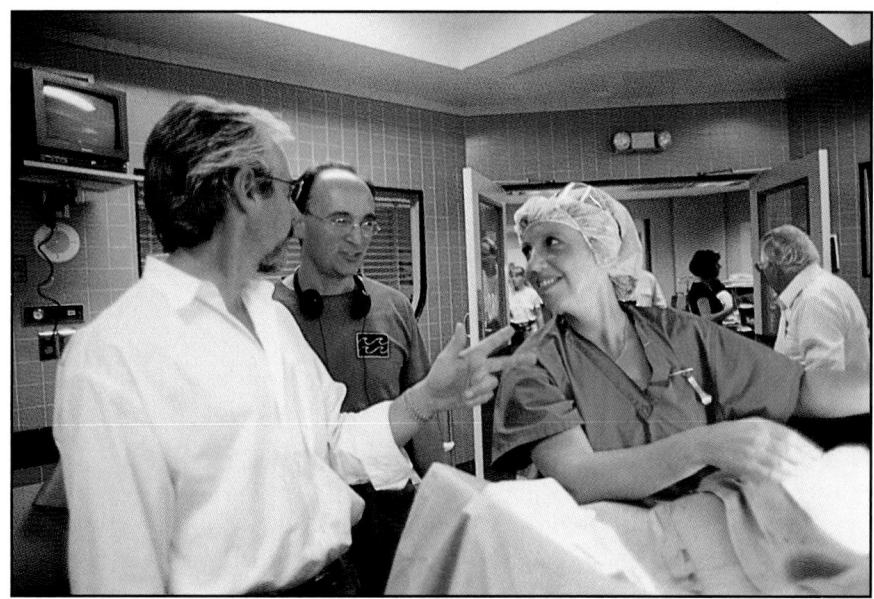

Dr. Lance Gentile, on-set technical adviser Dr. Joe Sachs, and Risa Stefani.

given to the writer, who uses the information to complete his or her scenes. Gentile also makes sure that the finalized script interprets the medicine correctly and that, once shot, it remains authentic all the way through the edited episode that will go on the air.

The character arcs and medical beats are crafted like a mosaic, with every writer contributing to every episode. Once individual episode assignments are given, the writer goes off, writes a six-page story outline, and brings it back to the group. As a group, the writers make notes and discuss it again. After the story issues have been resolved, the writer then writes a draft of the script and comes back to the group for more input. Despite this group approach, the individual writer's voice continues to echo through the script. "I don't believe that every script should be run through my typewriter to give it a unified voice," said Wells. "I think the show itself inspires a unified voice. I like the feeling of having separate artistic viewpoints—from the writers, and then from the directors, and then from the actors. I think it makes the show a little different, and keeps it from being homogenous, so that the audience doesn't always know what they're going to get when they turn it on."

But the writers do. "You have to know your personal stories," said Manning, "because the people who write after you are expecting you to lay that story pipe, or connection, so they can pick up the thread when it's time for them to write their script. And it's important to keep in mind what has been written, medically, in the episodes prior to yours. For example, it's better to have a different character handling the weighty life-and-death sort of story than the same one who handled it in the weeks before."

Occasionally, the writers will find themselves taking wrong creative turns during the scripting process and having to rework major plot lines. "You sometimes write something and decide to change it halfway through," said Manning. "For 'Sleepless in Chicago,' I started a story with Ross dealing directly with a little girl who was being burned on the hand by her mother. In the end, the mother reveals that she herself had been punished in the same way when she was a child. I got halfway through and realized Ross should not be the one handling this case at all. It should be Hathaway. Hathaway's personal story was that she was trying to become a foster parent to a little Russian girl and I knew that by the end of the episode she would be rejected because of her suicide attempt a year earlier. I had written almost the entire story when it came to me that it should be Hathaway who was passing judgment on this mother and who was instrumental in having the child taken away from her. It made more of an impact later on when Hathaway was told *she* was an unfit mother because she had tried to kill herself. That's a good example of how a medical story can be refracted in a couple different personal ways."

Crichton and Spielberg offer their notes throughout the writing process. "I proudly say that I enjoy reporting to John Wells," said Spielberg. "He's my boss. I have a very strong relationship with John in that I'll read the treatments and then the scripts and I'll give him ideas. He's free to use them and he's free to throw them away. I'm never insulted when nothing is used, and I'm always very pleased when something gets in there." During development, the scripts are also reviewed by Gentile and Baer. By the time a script is ready to go into production, it is medically correct.

This intricate system of checks and balances includes Sachs, who, once the writer has completed a script and it's been approved by Gentile, gives it the once-over for fine-tuning. "A script will come out and I will give notes in the early stages—things I think need to be tweaked or portrayed a little differently. Sometimes I might have knowledge of some newer drugs or procedures or technologies that would be nice to insert, and I'll mention them at this time."

Wells and the writers shape all the scripts as a group, but it's the individual writer's job to shade them—occasionally bending the medical reality for dramatic effect. "There are some stories I fight all the way," said Gentile. "For example, in one of the episodes Ross beats up a man who abused his daughter by kicking her out of an upstairs window. It was an unrealistic action for a doctor to take, but on the other hand, it was also very powerful. The writer, who happened to be John in this case, shaded it to make it as palatable to me as he could. It was a compromise. Some of the things the writers want to do dramatically make me want to have a seizure. They'll still do it, but they'll build into the scene apologies or reasons for the action to take place."

As a writer, Gentile finds himself struggling with the same kinds of dilemmas when it's his turn to face the printed page. "I fight these issues myself," he admitted. "I'll say, 'Lance, this is totally unrealistic, it's completely ridiculous.' 'Yeah, but it's such a great, powerful scene, I've got to have it.' And I'm supposed to be the voice of reason." Gentile dealt with this internal debate most dramatically when he wrote "Love's Labor Lost," in which a mother dies during a difficult childbirth. "This entire complicated obstetrical case was played out in the emergency room, which was completely and painfully unrealistic. And *I* wrote it. How can I tell the other writers not to do things in the emergency room when I've done the most flagrant thing myself? There was a lot of feedback from the public on that one, and I took a lot of heat for it, particularly from doctors."

A scene from the Emmy Award–winning episode, "Love's Labor Lost."

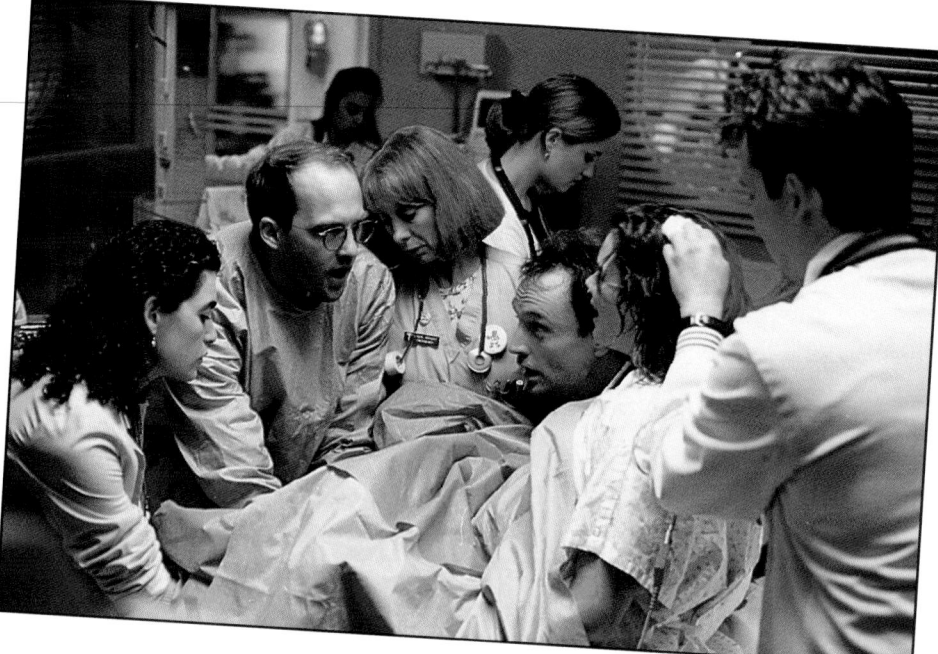

While the medical community has been quick to point out medical errors and inaccuracies, it has also been willing to acknowledge *ER* for its honesty and insights into the profession. The National Kidney Foundation presented a 1995 public service award to Neal Baer as writer of "The Gift," an episode that dealt with the sensitive issue of organ donation. The California Chapter of the American College of Emergency Physicians presented Gentile with the Media Award for 1995 as the person who did the most to promote the specialty of emergency medicine. "From the beginning of the series we decided to take liberties when necessary," said Gentile. "We knew there would be times when scenes would not depict exactly the way emergency medicine is practiced. But *ER* is a dramatic show, and on the measure, we are presenting this profession as a profession of heroes. I think that's what the public is going to take from it. We've done more to promote the emergency room specialty and make people aware of its problems and challenges than any other medium has done before. The audience is responding, and physicians are responding. I was at a medical convention where doctors came up to me and said, 'People now understand what I do for a living, the patients understand why they have to wait sometimes, and my *family* understands what I do. They never knew before.' "

WRITERS MEETING
WARNER BROS. STUDIOS, BURBANK
JUNE 13, 1995

On this quiet summer afternoon, the writers for *ER* are meeting in the conference room next to John Wells's office at Warner Bros. They have only recently returned from a brief hiatus following an exhausting and triumphant first season. After having spent the previous year working out their standards in writing, producing, and directing, they find themselves in the more comfortable position of building the second season upon an extremely successful foundation.

A long conference table is banked by the people who will decide the shape of the '95–'96 season. Present with Wells are Lance Gentile, Tracey Stern, Neal Baer, Paul Manning, Mimi Leder, Carol Flint, and Lydia Woodward. They chat informally for a few minutes, taking care of various housekeeping matters: episodes need to be offered as Emmy submissions; a master calendar of awards ceremonies and personal speaking engagements would be a good idea to keep everything straight. By the time Michael Crichton arrives and is seated next to Wells, such basic issues have been dealt with and the writers meeting begins in earnest.

John Wells (foreground) and the ER team at a studio writers meeting.

The conversation turns to the character arcs that serve as the foundation for the show's story lines. Large white dry-erase boards are mounted on two walls of the conference room with ideas for the first twelve episodes sketched out in color-coded ink. Under the heading for Episode One is listed: *Greene's 1st day as attending, Carter's 1st day back, new medical students.* A third, free-standing board details character turns by name: Greene, Ross, Lewis, Hathaway, Benton, Carter, and Boulet each head a column under which are written possibilities for individual character experiences. Beneath "Greene" are the cryptic phrases: *embarrassed at Jennifer's work; commuter flirtation; has what he wants—now what?*

Plotting character development.

Today there is much discussion about Dr. Susan Lewis's quirky and irrepressible sister Chloe, who had a baby at the end of the previous season. What will happen with Chloe and the baby during the first six episodes of Season Two? It is a question made urgent by the real-life pregnancy of Kathleen Wilhoite, the actress who plays Chloe. Because of this, Chloe needs to be gone from the drama—for whatever reason—within a couple of months, and the writers are faced with finding an immediate story solution.

While that much is clear, there is little else obvious this afternoon. Various options are considered. What if Chloe ends up in jail? What if she gets it together, goes back to school, and gets a job? Should she leave the baby with Lewis? Should she take the baby with her when she goes? All possible story lines—complete with character analyses—are explored at length. Chloe becomes a real person, with real motivations. She is spoken of with such familiar insight that she begins to glimmer with life before the writers at the table.

By seven the writers have finished for the day. The fate of Chloe and her baby is still undetermined, but the writers are further along in thinking it through, and a few more pieces of a very complicated plot puzzle have been placed. They will return to this table many times over the next few weeks before facing their own keyboards and scripting the stories they have collectively begun to tell.

Chapter 3
Production

The pace is frenetic. Gurneys shoot through swinging doors as EMTs pound out the staccato beat of vital statistics. Doctors and nurses pick up the pace, and an injured patient is wheeled into a cacophonous trauma room. In a kaleidoscope of light and sound, the patient is transferred to the examination table on a three-count. Clothing is stripped off. An IV needle is inserted. Blood pressure is pumped and measured. Physicians trumpet stanzas of drug dosages and order diagnostic tests—and a chorus of medical personnel moves in carefully ordered chaos.

Where nothing is left to chance.

Making *ER* is not unlike the fast-paced, tightly organized teamwork played out on television every Thursday night. Each episode requires the exhaustive efforts of more than a hundred behind-the-scenes players who make sure every detail of this highly detailed drama is as authentic as possible. Like a real emergency room, it is not a milieu for the faint of heart.

Production of *ER* is organized around an overlapping schedule that, once the season starts shooting in July, doesn't stop until the following May. Every show is built on seven days of preparation, eight days of filming, and five days of postproduction editing and sound mixing. But *pre*production for one episode overlaps with the production phase of another episode, which overlaps with the *post*production phase of yet another. Everything, quite literally, happens at once.

"As soon as production starts, it's like jumping onto a conveyor belt headed for a shredder," Lydia Woodward admitted. "Every ninth day we have to have a new script, a new director, and a new cast ready to go.

It's really tough. When we started the show the first season, we were on a seven-day shooting schedule and, quite simply, we had trouble making it. That was because we were still discovering the show and because the pace of the show was so extremely fast, episodes were coming in five or six minutes short—which was a nightmare. We would end up having to shoot an additional day. Once the show went on the air and became a success, we were able to switch to an eight-day shoot, and by shooting eleven- or twelve-hour days, we pretty much finished the rest of the episodes on schedule."

ER requires a different director for every episode. With the frantic pace and overlapping scheduling, it would be physically impossible for one individual to be on stage creatively supervising a show while listening to actors audition for another, while at the same time sitting in the editing bay piecing together images from a different episode altogether. The roster of highly respected *ER* directors is headed by Mimi Leder, who directed six of the first season's episodes.

Production begins with a "concept meeting" the day a completed script comes out. Although the script may still undergo some adjustments after this point, its basic structure is developed enough for the key production personnel to see what will be needed for the episode. The production designer, costume designer, and

The pace and teamwork of a real emergency room are duplicated on the set of ER.

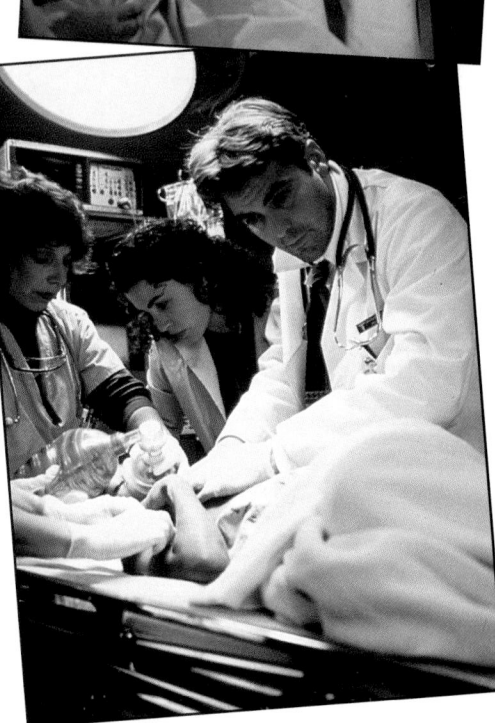

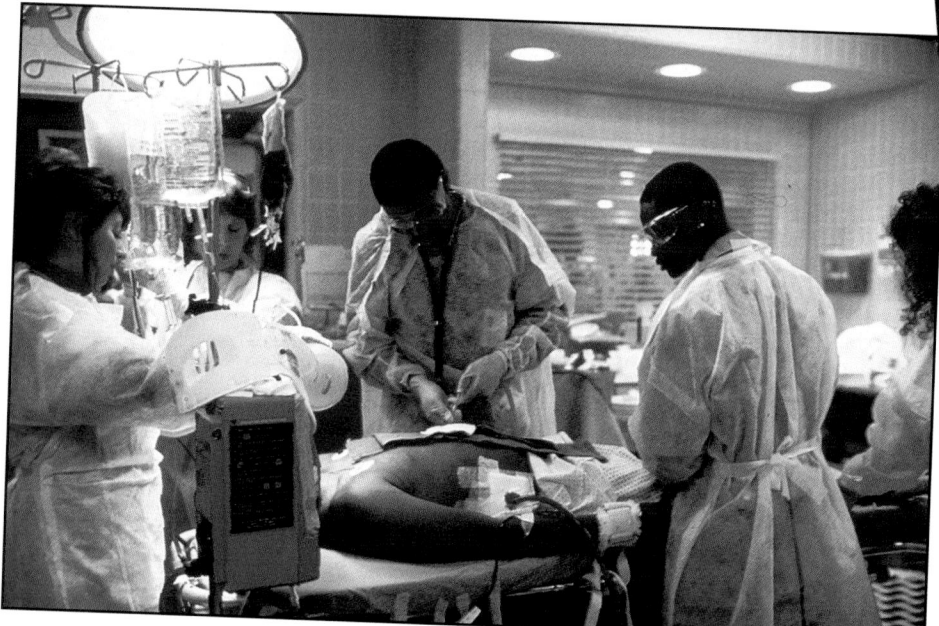

property masters meet with Wells, Woodward, and the episode director to roughly determine what will be physically necessary to produce the show.

The next step is a separate "tone meeting," where the director gets together with the writer and one of the producers to gain a better understanding of the idiosyncrasies of *ER* production. During the tone meeting, the writer goes through each scene with the director prior to filming. "As writers and producers, we find it essential to meet with the director beforehand," said Woodward. "Some of our directors are from the outside. They may not have done an *ER* before and they might not be familiar with the cast and crew. The tone meetings give the directors a head start in terms of their relationships with the actors and the production."

The tone meetings are also useful in clarifying the trajectory of the script. "We have directors of very high caliber working on *ER*," said Leder, "and we would never tell a director to direct in any certain way. We just want to be very clear about the tone of the scenes: where the characters are going, where they've been, and what they've gone through that has led them to this moment. A visiting director needs to be brought up to date with those kinds of issues."

Tone meetings are followed by production meetings, which are similar to the earlier concept meetings, but on a much larger scale. Production meetings include the producers, the director, and all the department heads as every possible requirement is discussed: cine-

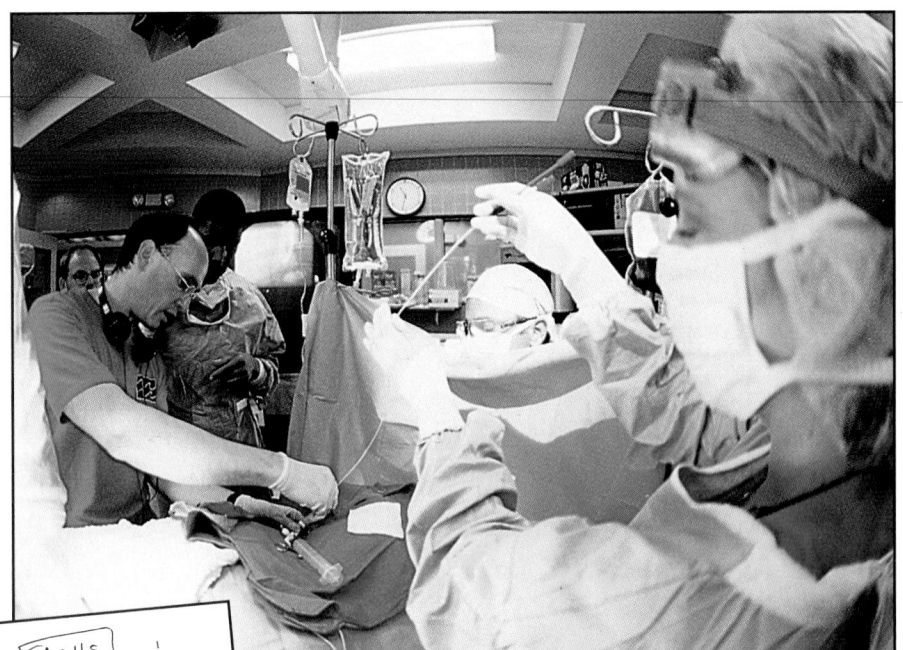

Dr. Joe Sachs shows Eriq La Salle a medical technique.

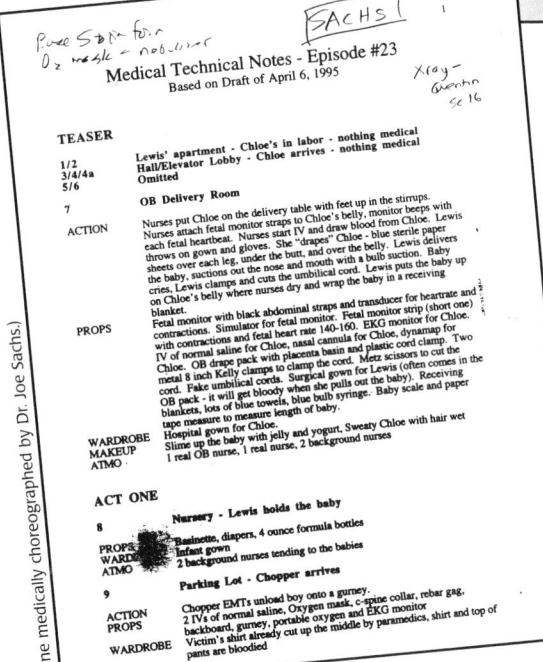

(Scene medically choreographed by Dr. Joe Sachs.)

matography, transportation, hair, makeup, costumes, sets, props, accounting, special effects, and so on. The script is read aloud and the specifics for every scene are thoroughly discussed. For example, if a scene describes Greene and Lewis in the doctors' lounge talking as they are taking food out of the refrigerator, it means the doctors' lounge set will be need to be prepared; food will have to be placed in the refrigerator beforehand; costumes and makeup will be need to be arranged for the actors; and Anthony Edwards and Sherry Stringfield will have to be notified of the specific day and time they will need to arrive at the studio. Even the simplest scenes require highly regimented organization. Understandably, those that indicate a serious medical trauma demand even more exacting attention.

Dr. Joe Sachs prepares notes for all scenes involving medical action to assist actors, makeup and props technicians, and other departments.

To assist with this, Joe Sachs prepares a medical/technical breakdown detailing the action, props, wardrobe, and makeup required for all scenes involving medical action. He also makes a note of whatever atmosphere or background movement will lend authenticity to the scene. Like Lance Gentile, Sachs is an emergency room physician with a film school degree (from Stanford instead of USC) and a longtime interest in moviemaking. Although he now devotes sixteen-hour days to the *ER* set, Sachs remains

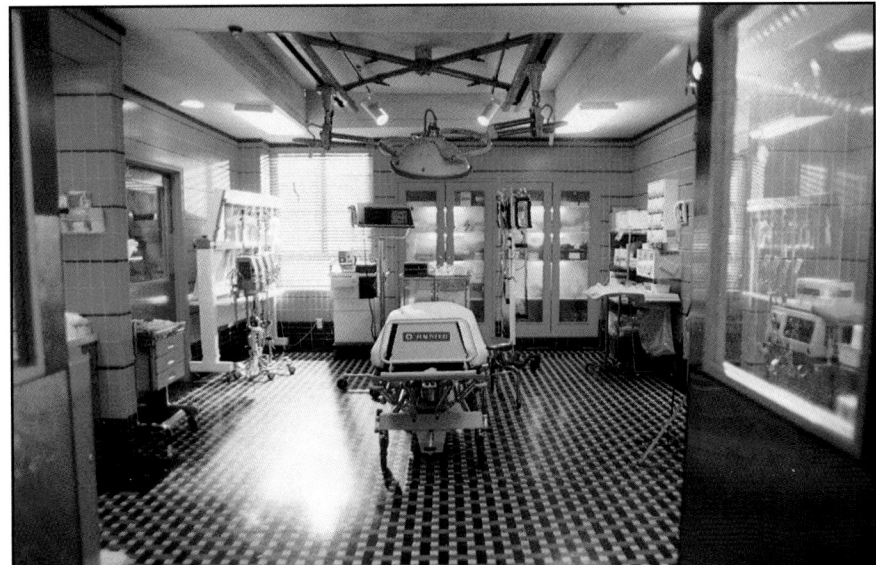

Authentic hard-wall set lends a perceptible sense of reality to ER.

on the clinical faculty at UCLA and a partner in an emergency group at Northridge Hospital Medical Center, where he continues to work at least one eight-hour shift per weekend. His medical/technical breakdown goes to the various departments at least a week before the shoot.

ER's hard-wall, closed-ceiling emergency room sets require advance preparation prior to filming and add another intrinsic element to the show's realism. The sets, many of which are permanent structures built on sound stages at Warner Bros., are constructed to look like real hospital interiors, as opposed to the more traditional stage settings sometimes used in television and film. Traditional sets are built with three walls, rather than four, leaving one side open to permit easy access for lighting, sound, and camera equipment. Cameras are basically aimed in a forward direction, much like the eyes of an audience facing a stage, with side shots and close-ups factored in accordingly. These sets are further equipped with an open ceiling, and once again, camera angles are carefully aligned to avoid revealing the lights and rafters that hang above. While watching shows filmed on these stages, the audience will frequently register a subliminal perception of theatricality. To establish the sense of reality so important to ER, the use of the authentic hard-wall sets was clearly mandated.

"It is much harder to move around on these stages because of the ceilings and walls that don't move," commented Leder, "but that's what makes you feel like you are really in the ER. The sets provide more interesting possibilities for us to choreograph scenes the way we do. We can shoot low and aim the camera up and see the great ceilings and architecture, or wind around the multilayered hallways. It's the only way to go. You feel a sense of reality and immediacy, as if you are really there. You feel like you're part of the action and that you want to be with these people. I think it's a very subconscious thing, but I think it's one of the keys to the show."

The show's emergency room sets follow the same basic design established in the pilot, but are laid out somewhat differently to make better use of the stage space. Their patterns and colors are identical to those at the Linda Vista Hospital location. The hospital sets are meticulously dressed with items from real life by set decorator Michael Claypool and crew. Medical furnishings and equipment fill every room. Even the drawers and cupboards contain genuine medical supplies. Claypool works directly with production designer Ivo Cristante, who plans and designs all the sets for the show, and construction coordinator Bob Parker, who is responsible for making sure they are built to Cristante's specifications.

Stage 11 measures one hundred feet in length and one hundred thirty feet in width, with almost the entire area covered with permanent sets. The ambulance entrance, the treatment and trauma rooms, the main hallway, the elevator, the admissions desk, the X-ray room, the doctors' lounge, the suture room, the stairwell, and the familiar room at the end of the hall where the doctors are frequently caught napping—all are carefully packed into 9,705 square feet of space.

Director of photography Richard Thorpe adjusts lighting.

"There isn't a lot of room that we don't use on stage," said Christopher Chulack, who oversees all areas of production and directs two episodes a season. "The set basically fills the entire space, which makes it very tight to be on for twelve hours a day. It's not unusual to have a hundred people on the set on any given

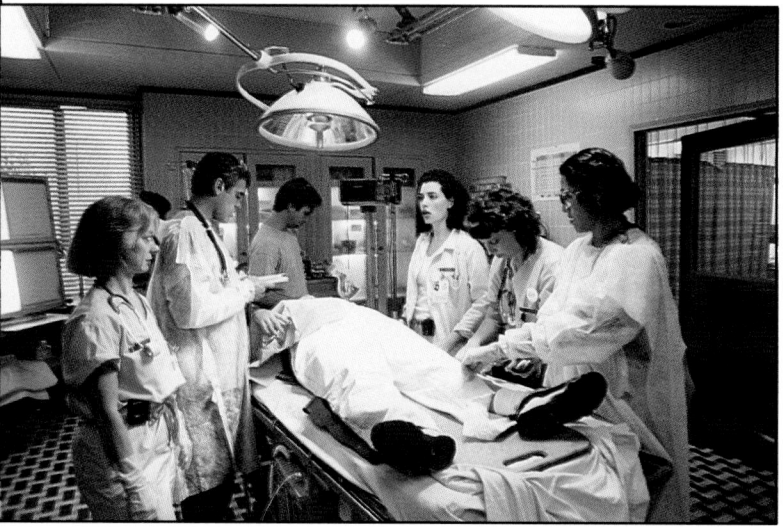

Use of creative and realistic lighting designs contributes to ER's authenticity.

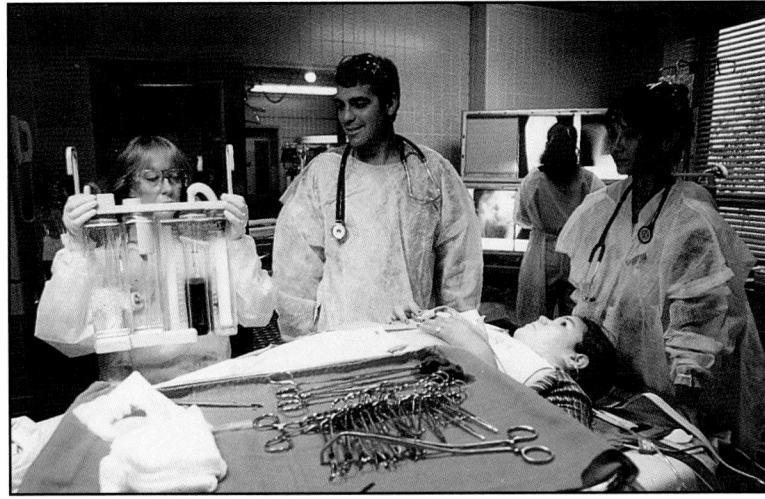

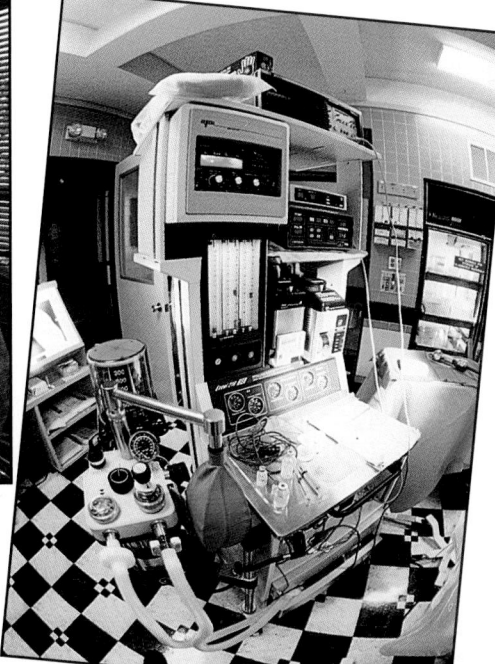

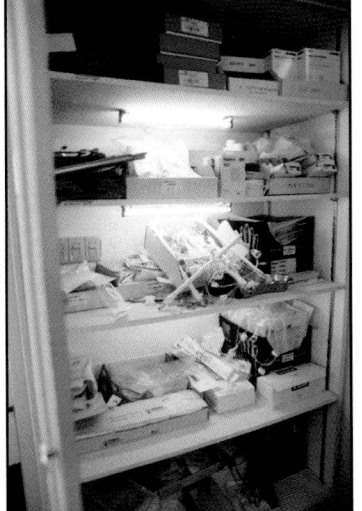

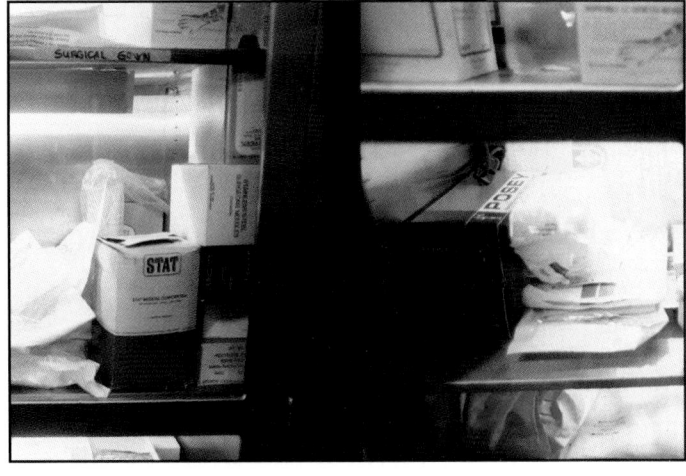

Set director Michael Claypool and staff make sure that rooms and cabinets are stocked with real-life medical supplies, and that the necessary O.R. equipment is in place.

day. It can get very intense, especially because—with the hard ceilings—the sound doesn't go out. It's kind of like a submarine. The first few weeks of the mission are fine, but by about the second month, patience wears thin."

Stage 3 at Warner Bros. is somewhat smaller than Stage 11 and houses the operating room, the ER waiting room, the hospital cafeteria, and other hospital departments, such as the new childcare facility added at the beginning of the second season. During the first season it also contained the apartments for the show's main characters, which were built and struck as necessary.

A third stage, Stage 2, was added during the second season as a "swing stage," allowing the production company to build temporary

Director of photography Richard Thorpe.

sets, such as apartments or other locations, as called for on an episode-by-episode basis. As with the hospital sets, Claypool and crew make sure these other sets are dressed with an assortment of items from everyday life.

As part of his lighting design for the sets, director of photography Richard Thorpe uses the fluorescent lights that are wired—like those in a real hospital room—to turn on with the flick of a wall switch. "The problem with pre-lit sets," he said, "is that all the light comes from the top. That tends to make people look a little 'raccoonish.' We like to augment the overhead light with lights on the floor or the sides whenever we can, but because of the nature of the way that *ER* is shot— with the Steadicam moving much of the time—it can sometimes become a challenge to conceal those lights as the camera goes by. We're limited in what we can do. Having the set pre-lit makes the job easier in some ways, but more difficult in other situations. On our practical sets we can't remove walls to position lights or get a better camera angle." Despite the limitations, the overall effect of the lighting works to the show's advantage by heightening the authenticity of the setting.

In other cases, Thorpe uses creative techniques to augment the lighting by suggesting a natural light source. "It's always been my style to add light coming from sources through windows," he said, "so if we're

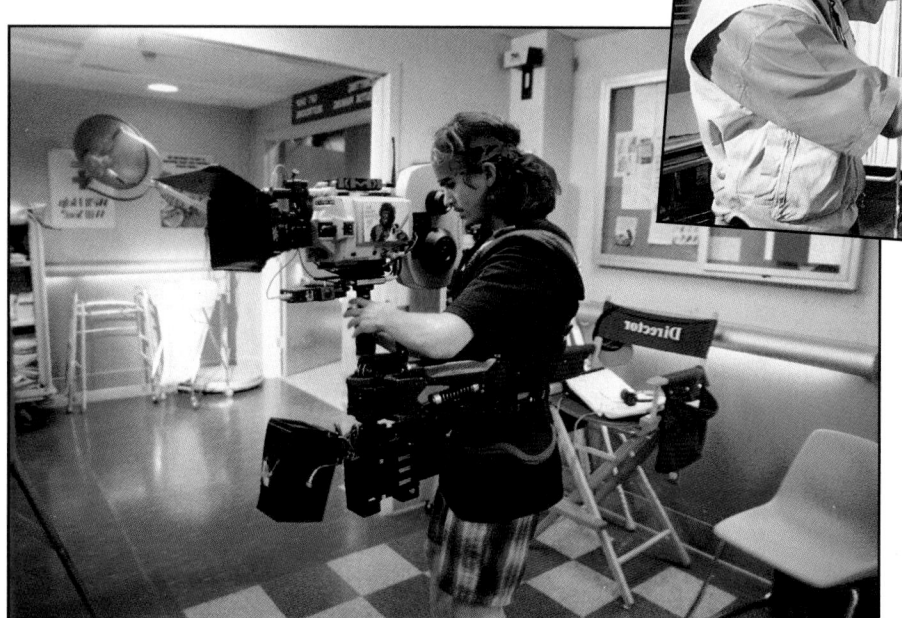

Gaffer Joe Capshaw checks light reading.

Steadicam operator Guy Norman Bee.

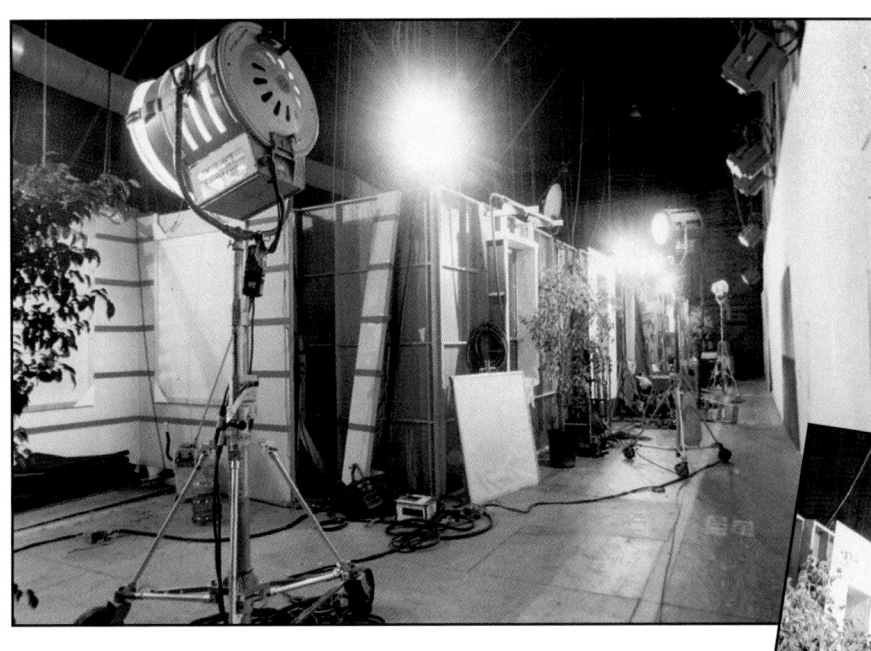

Creating the effect of natural lighting coming in through set windows.

doing day scenes, for example, we have nice hot sunlight coming into the room. For night scenes, we put some twinkle lights outside to give it a little bit of depth in the dark. The reality, of course, is always that there's just a stage wall there, but we try to make it seem as though we're in a big city like Chicago." Special effects supervisor Scott Forbes further enhances this reality with the atmospheric elements of rain, snow, and wind as called for by the script.

Although a few exteriors were shot on the Warner Bros. back lot during the first season—the doctors' basketball court and the snow scenes from "Blizzard," for example—most of the exteriors were shot on location in Chicago. This added realism to the show, but created considerable story and filming restrictions. Every time the writers wanted to move the action outside County General they had to either limit their concepts or wait until the next trip to Chicago. "It didn't make sense to go to Chicago to shoot against a brick wall at an ambulance entrance," John Wells noted. "We wanted to be able to use our time there to shoot the real exteriors we

A Chicago blizzard can be re-created on the Warner Bros. back lot.

Set director
Michael Claypool and
production designer
Ivo Cristante creat-
ing new ER sets.

Two views of the
new exterior set of
the ambulance
entrance.

couldn't get anywhere else—Lake Michigan, the downtown area, and the El track. Building some of the hospital exteriors on the back lot was just a better use of our time."

For the second season, Cristante designed an exterior courtyard that was built as an ambulance entrance to match the interior ambulance drive-up on Stage 11. Additionally, a front façade of County General was constructed on "New York Street" on the Warner Bros. back lot. "The exterior of the hospital is a typical 1950s building," said Cristante, "part brick and part glass, very similar to many hospitals with an old wing and a new wing married together." An elevated train track was also constructed, along with a diner-style restaurant. "We basically built the environs around the hospital. The big trick was to make sure we don't see any trees because many of the episodes will take place in the wintertime in Chicago—and all the trees at Warner Bros. are deciduous."

Clearly, mounting a production as elaborate and multilayered as *ER* requires a highly focused and dedicated crew. Shooting the extremely dense seventy-page scripts in just eight days—and paying proper attention to the technical aspects and the dramatics—is a monumental undertaking. "It gets pretty crazy," said Chulack. "But in theory, we try to let the frenetic pace of the show carry over to the shooting pace. It doesn't always work and people get tired. *ER* is a challenging show; it's one of the toughest shows I've ever produced from both an emotional and a physical standpoint. But the writing is so terrific we want to make sure the production lives up to it." With Chulack heading up physical production and unit production manager Mike Salamunovich managing the fiscal logistics, the fifty-person crew works hard to do just that.

Producer Christopher Chulack.

ER employs five assistant directors who support the episode directors by taking care of myriad production details. First assistant directors T. R. "Babs" Subramaniam and Tommy Burns work alternating episodes—each in turn assisting a director through both the preproduction and production phases. They help the director break down the script and work out a schedule for the shoot. Subramaniam and Burns also serve as coordinators between the director and the other departments. Once shooting begins, they are responsible for making sure the carefully laid plans actually come to pass on the set.

Three second assistant directors make up the rest of the AD team. Key second assistant director Michael

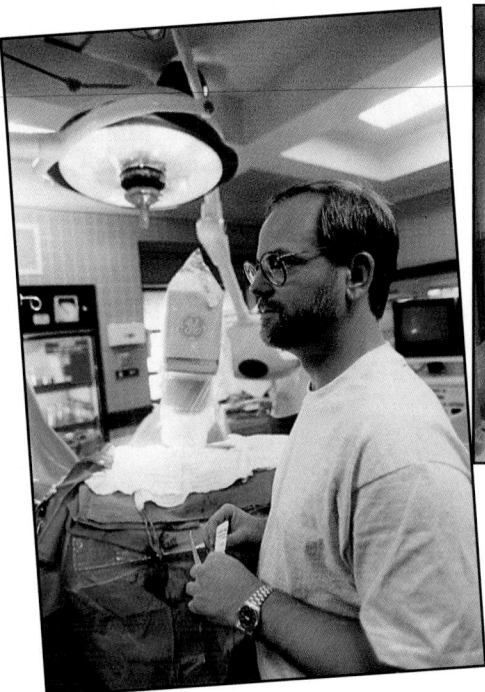

Key second assistant director Michael Pendell, whose duties include hiring and directing extras and preparing *ER*'s daily "call sheet."

Pendell works every show and is charged with scheduling and making out the "call sheet" that informs the cast and crew of each day's shoot. The call sheet lists the date, times, sets, pages of the script to be covered, location, actors, crew members, makeup call times, and numerous other details vital to the smooth operation of the show.

Pendell is also in charge of the extras: hiring them, supervising them, and directing them as part of *ER*'s realistic atmosphere. He works with Central Casting Services in scheduling an average of thirty-five individuals each day who appear on the set as nurses, orderlies, paramedics, clerks, patients, and housekeeping personnel. Some of the extras come back every day, including four who serve as stand-ins for the principal actors during lighting sessions. Often one or two real-life nurses are hired to work the trauma scenes. Their skilled presence is useful to Sachs in blocking the scenes, as well as to the show's regular medical cast, who frequently work alongside them passing various instruments and setting up emergency treatment like professionals.

Between shots, the extras stay in an offstage holding area with second second assistant director Chris Salamunovich, who oversees their arrival in the morning and makes sure they're ready to perform throughout the day. He also helps Pendell with other second AD

Off-camera advisers, technicians, and extras.

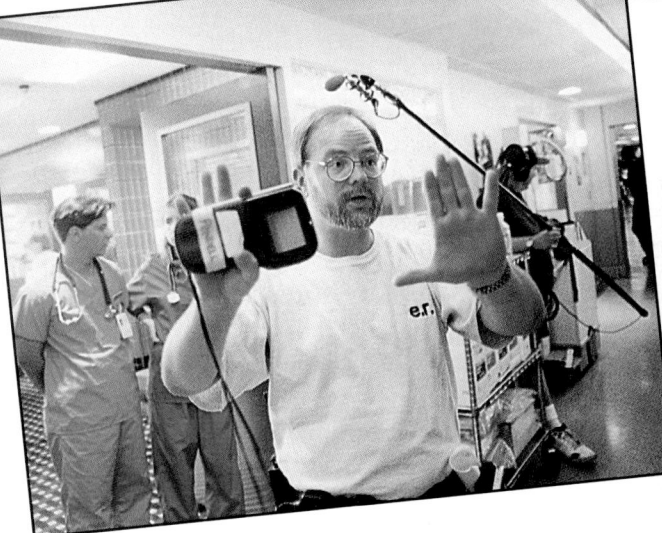

duties to allow Pendell enough time to direct the extras in the background of scenes. "The hardest part of my job is making the hospital look busy every moment," said Pendell. "With all its windows and doors—and only thirty-five people—that's difficult to do, especially on the long Steadicam shots that look in several different directions during one take."

Pendell uses a small handheld TV monitor that picks up a broadcast of the same images that play on the director's video monitor. Based on that information and long experience, he can watch the principal actors as they rehearse and know ahead of time exactly where extras will be seen. By carefully moving people around and alternating players, the same extras can be used again and again. "Normally I would have people change costumes between setups to make them seem like different

Michael Pendell places his background extras after monitoring principal actors' rehearsal on a minicamera.

Makeup artist
Werner Keppler pre-
pares Christine
Elise for a scene.

characters," he said, "but we don't have the time for that. This production moves so fast, we'd be shooting the next scene before they could even get into their costumes." By the time the director has finished rehearsing, Pendell has the extras in position and ready to move on cue.

Additional second assistant director Catherine Bond spends her day keeping track of the principal actors, or "first team," as they are called. Bond makes sure they get through the costume, hair, and makeup departments and are on stage in plenty of time for their scenes. She does the same for the numerous day players and guest stars who are on the set for as much as one or two days at a time—or for as little as one or two scenes.

As with the pilot, the challenge of casting the dozens of guest stars and day players who appear each week on *ER* is met by Barbara Miller and John Levey. Because the job is so large, Levey works exclusively for *ER*, as opposed to other studio casting directors who may handle several different shows at the same time. The reason for this is understandable. The average tally for an hour-long drama is ten speaking parts in addition to the series regulars; *ER* often requires between twenty-five and thirty-five for every episode. "The casting director's nightmare is that someone will say, 'Action,' and there won't be anybody there," admitted Levey. "Fortunately, that's never happened." To avoid this, Levey auditioned nearly five thousand actors during the first season, ultimately casting close to four hundred individuals for a variety of parts. Almost 80 percent of all the parts on *ER* are filled by day players who, as the name implies, are character actors who work on the show for a single day playing a minor role.

The authenticity of *ER* is further enhanced by making sure the actors hired as patients or medical staff look like real people. "Sometimes it's fun to cast a glamorous show," said Levey, "where everybody is fifty times better looking than people are in reality. But *ER* takes place in Chicago, which is filled with people who have come from all over the world, who are too tall and too short, too fat and too thin—and who look like hell because they are sick. Or feel like hell because somebody they care about is sick. None of us are at our stylish best when we're in the ER. That's not the story we're after."

For Levey, the most difficult parts to cast are the EMTs. "Those guys have to push gurneys at forty miles an hour while saying, 'BP one-forty over ninety, tachy at one-sixty, gave him three hundred cc's of saline!'

Carlos Gomez and Ron Eldard as ER's EMTs.

That's really hard—most people can't say that stuff sitting still, much less running down the hallway. The actors have to go in very prepared or we can lose a lot of time on the set. One of my favorite moments in casting is when we'll ask an actor if he has any questions. And he'll say, 'Yeah, how do you say "anaphylactic"?' We'll tell him: 'With authority.' Because we don't know either."

During the second season Gloria Reuben, who had portrayed physical therapist Jeanie Boulet during the latter part of the first season, joined the *ER* cast as a regular. Other actors were introduced as guest stars to appear throughout several episodes, including Ron Eldard as EMT Ray Shepherd; Christine Elise as medical student Harper Tracy; and Laura Innes as new chief resident Dr. Kerry Weaver. "Characters are introduced to the show for very specific story reasons," said John Wells. "For instance, the second season we wrote in Dr. Kerry Weaver because we needed a new chief resident. We were trying to stay true to an authentic sequence of medical training, and Dr. Greene had moved from being chief resident to becoming an attending physician at the hospital. The way we had set up the story in the first season, none of the other characters could fill that role. We will also create a new character if we need one to interact with one of our major characters, like a new love interest, for example. If that character becomes someone we have a lot to write about, then we make that person a regular on the cast. That's what happened with Jeanie Boulet, who came back the second season involved with Benton."

Costuming the characters is another production essential. The task of making sure every performer on *ER* is properly attired is headed up

Gloria Reuben as Jeanie Boulet.

ON THE SET
WARNER BROS. STUDIOS, BURBANK
AUGUST 4, 1995

The cool darkness around the perimeter of Stage 11 gives way to the colorful tile and fluorescent lighting of the *ER* set. Extras—some wearing uniforms, others dressed in street clothes or hospital gowns—silently haunt the hallways and treatment rooms, making sure to keep clear of the emergency being staged within the familiar yellow-tiled walls of Trauma 1. They are well practiced at disappearing into the woodwork whenever the stage bell rings to alert the company of the camera's impending roll. By the time director Eric Laneuville says, "Action," they have become invisible.

Second AD Mike Pendell has hired thirty-five extras for today's shoot. Many of them have been here before and handle the wheelchairs and IV carts like seasoned veterans. Their background presence is an essential element of the hospital setting. Although only a few extras are needed for the frenetic trauma scene now being filmed, *all* were required for sequences shot earlier this morning when Pendell directed them in precisely timed and perfectly repeated background energy every time the camera rolled. After this trauma room setup, Pendell will redirect the extras again and again, making thirty-five seem more like two hundred as the day progresses.

The trauma scene—featuring a teenage football player (Victor D. Castro) who has been slammed in the solar plexus—is also perfectly repeated time after time. Anthony Edwards plays opposite Laura Innes, who has joined the cast as new chief resident Dr. Kerry Weaver. They are

Laura Innes as Dr. Kerry Weaver.

Yvette Freeman as Nurse Haleh Adams.

surrounded by several of the series regulars and a team of extras, including a real-life nurse whose medical training lends efficiency and expertise to the drama.

The medical emergency was blocked in fits and starts by on-set technical adviser Joe Sachs prior to the shoot. While Laneuville was focused on capturing separate footage of the principal actors in one of the hallways, Sachs took the trauma scene players aside and quickly put them through their paces one at a time. Yvette Freeman, who plays Nurse Haleh Adams, took meticulous notes on her "sides" (the miniaturized portion of the script that contains this particular scene) as Sachs directed her movements in coordination with the lines. She carefully studied the notes offstage prior to the shoot. The script had been revised the night before and the last-minute adjustments caused the cast to focus more attention than usual on their dialogue.

The scene is embellished by a soft rain falling outside the windows of Trauma 1. Special effects supervisor Scott Forbes has prepared a long, narrow sprinkler with hoses that are turned on and off for every take. A basin collects the water, and pipes carry the flow away from the set. The sound of the rain is barely perceptible on stage, however, and will be added to the scene later on in postproduction.

The A-camera is filming from just outside the trauma room's windowed doors. The actors pick up the pace of the scene until it chugs like an accelerating locomotive. Laneuville finally gets the take he is after and calls, "Cut! Print!" The company relaxes for a moment, smiling and joking after the intensity of the drama. They don't go very far, however. Within minutes they will begin replaying the drama for the Steadicam.

Polinsky and Dr.
Joe Sachs prepare
an extra's wardrobe
for a trauma scene.

by costume designer Lyn Paolo, who works with costume supervisor Doris Alaimo. Key costumer Steven Zimbelman assists Paolo and Alaimo, and costumers Radford Polinsky and Eden Coblenz manage wardrobe on the set.

As with every other element on *ER*, the job of costuming the show presents a formidable challenge. An average script might dictate twenty or thirty different costumes per episode with more elaborate episodes demanding even more. The second season opener, "Welcome Back, Carter," required costumes for forty-two characters plus miscellaneous trauma victims, some of whom required duplicate wardrobe items because their clothing was deliberately cut off or damaged during shooting. In addition to this, every episode includes the atmosphere players, who wear a variety of outfits on the set. For major street or disaster scenes, as many as seventy-five atmosphere players may require outfitting in addition to the principal and guest actors.

Close-up of
Polinsky's vest—
filled with a
wardrober's emer-
gency tools.

ER's kinetic emergency room activity is anything but random. All scenes are carefully planned in advance by the director, who, most typically, will meet with Joe Sachs several days prior to shooting to prepare for the intricate trauma or critical care scenes. Together they discuss where all the principal characters are going to be for a scene and determine whether or not the blocking will work technically. The next step is to plan the remaining activity in the room. "Blocking these scenes is as complicated as choreographing a ballet," Sachs explained. "And it's all cued to dialogue. For example, if Benton is saying, 'Tracheal shift and hyperresonant on the left,' he is, at the same time, percussing—or tapping—the chest, which I teach him how to do. When he says, 'Tension pneumo,' he takes the stethoscope and listens." For almost every line of dialogue, there is accompanying action. "The trick is that we are going to do six takes of the scene from eight different angles—and the action has to be done the same way every time. It takes a lot of concentration."

As a director, Mimi Leder finds this practice particularly useful in understanding the medical terminology and intent of the blocking. "I begin by asking questions," she said. "I often don't know what a certain procedure means, and I certainly don't know how to do it, but Joe does. I tell him how I'd like the scene to go. He tells me how it *should* go. I then decide on camera angles. I may want a character to cross around and come through a certain door to take me to another shot. I need to make sure that makes sense medically. Would he really do that? You

A page of script and Dr. Joe Sachs's accompanying "blocking" for the actors.

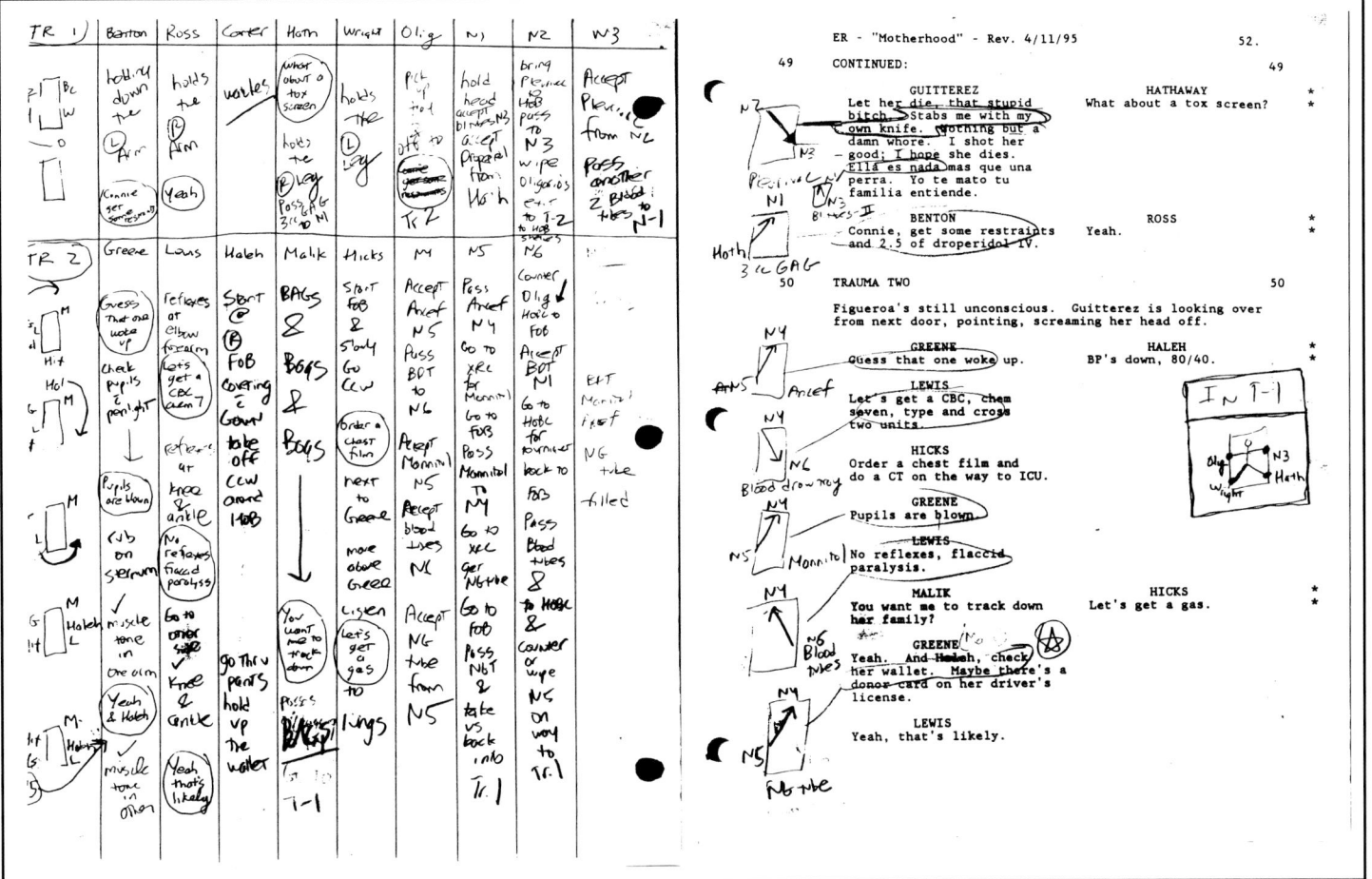

(Scene medically choreographed by Dr. Joe Sachs.)

have to talk about it and figure it out ahead of time. We take dramatic license sometimes, but not that often. I think we're fairly accurate with our procedures. We always try to figure out a way to do them accurately *and* cinematically."

For every page of script involving a trauma scene, Sachs spends a minimum of one hour the night before working through the complicated choreography that involves as many as twenty different people moving in twenty different directions. Opposite every page of dialogue, he writes columns of blocking for each character detailing the specific action to be taken throughout the scene. Every movement is very meticulously blocked out. "Some people have said *ER* is just guerrilla filmmaking." He laughed. "They think we just set up the camera and the actors run around the bed and we get whatever we can. The fact is, every detail that goes on the screen is carefully planned." Sachs also draws a bird's-eye view map of the trauma rooms for the prop department showing the patient lying center stage on a gurney and the location of all the medical props required for the scene.

Prop masters Beverly Hadley and Rick Kerns, who supervise alternating shows to accommodate overlapping preparation and production periods, work with assistant prop master Rick Ladomade in obtaining and supervising the thousands of props that are used each season on *ER*. Computers, beds, stethoscopes, X-ray screens, heart mon-

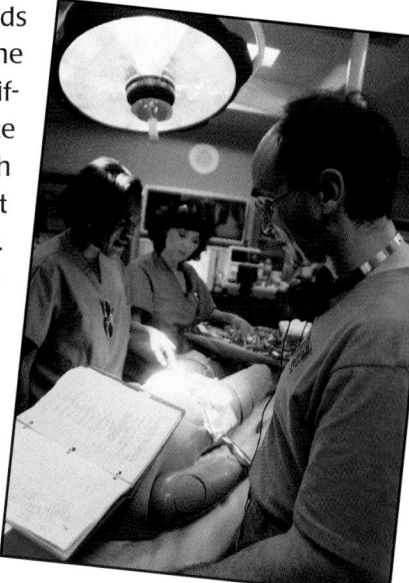

CCH Pounder, Risa Stefani, and Dr. Sachs work on medical choreography.

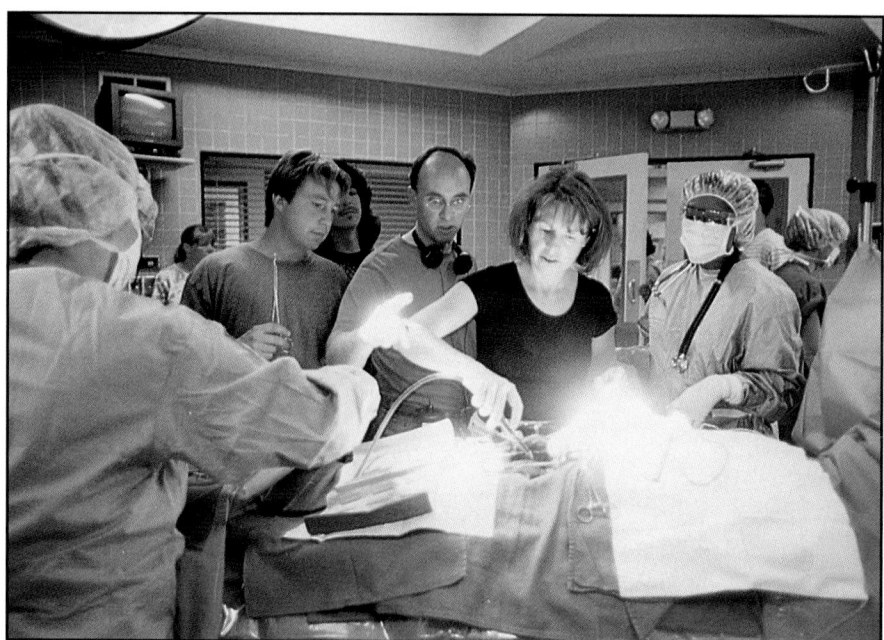

Assistant prop master Rick Ladomade, Dr. Sachs, and prop master Beverly Hadley setting up for surgery.

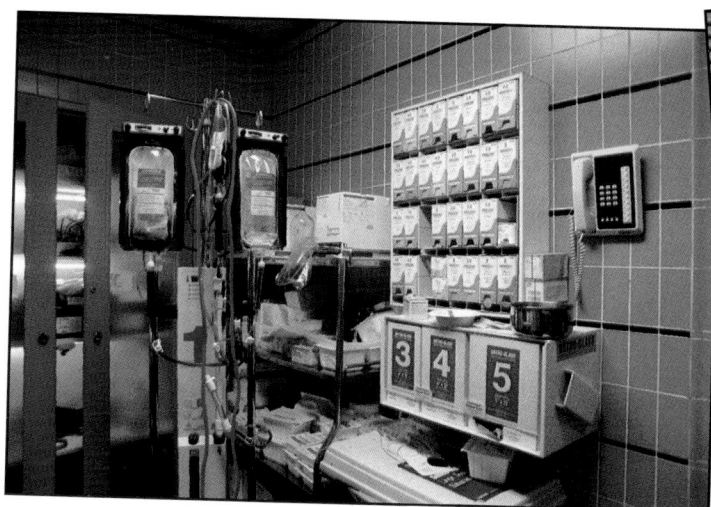

Genuine hospital supplies and machinery—even a doctor's actual clipboard—are used on the set.

itors, rubber gloves, suture trays, and bandages are among the hundreds of different items used on every episode—all of which have been donated by manufacturers. The prop crew makes sure the materials are always used correctly. "Our job is to make sure everything looks as real and accurate as possible," said Ladomade. "Any time a patient is hooked up to a breathing machine or an EKG, we make sure they're properly connected to the equipment. It's part of what makes the scene look real to the audience. You wouldn't want to see somebody lying in a bed with an IV that's not really going into their skin or a nasal cannula sticking out." The *ER* prop department is so dedicated to detail that they even type authentic charts for the clipboards the actors carry around on stage.

Brand-name containers and authentic packaging for drugs are always used, as well—minus their original contents. "As a prop crew," said Kerns, "Rick, Beverly, and I have always felt that 'Greeked' labels are much more distracting than real ones." "Greeking" is an old term that comes from the practice of altering familiar brand names by changing the letters so they look something like the symbols of the Greek alphabet while retaining the basic colors and shape of the original product design. "The audience may not notice the real stuff, but they do notice when it's Greeked. It's very distracting."

Not all props are readily available from medical supply companies, however. For some medical scenes, props may require modification to create the illusion of functioning in a realistic way. For example, trick syringes are spring-loaded so that a blunted needle retracts into the

The magical efforts of the props department: trick syringe and scalpel.

casing while it appears to be injected into the skin of a patient. The prop department keeps them in assorted sizes by the drawerful. Gag surgical knives are another standard item. Although it appears to be making a cut, the trick scalpel is actually pumping a slender trail of "blood" onto the patient from a minuscule hole in its tip.

More elaborate traumas require considerably greater advance preparation and rigging. A particularly busy sequence might require as many as one hundred and fifty different props. For serious traumas where *ER* doctors appear to be cracking a patient's chest, for example, an articulated (poseable) dummy equipped with a side of real animal ribs is actually used. To do this, the makeup department supplies the prop crew with fake latex skin that is used to cover the dummy patient's chest. A hole is cut and the ribs are placed inside. When dressed with surgical drapes and carefully photographed, the effect looks exactly as if the doctor is cutting into someone's chest and spreading the ribs to massage the heart.

Kerns gives a lot of the credit to *ER*'s talented ensemble for making the illusion of emergency medical care read realistically on film. "We couldn't work this smoothly if it weren't for the actors," he said. "They're all very good with the medical props. And they have improved as the show's progressed. They really have a knack for it now. It's rewarding to set up one of these traumas, and then sit back and watch the monitor as the actors do a switch off from a long tube to a short tube as the camera slides behind somebody. You can't see them do it, and you're sure

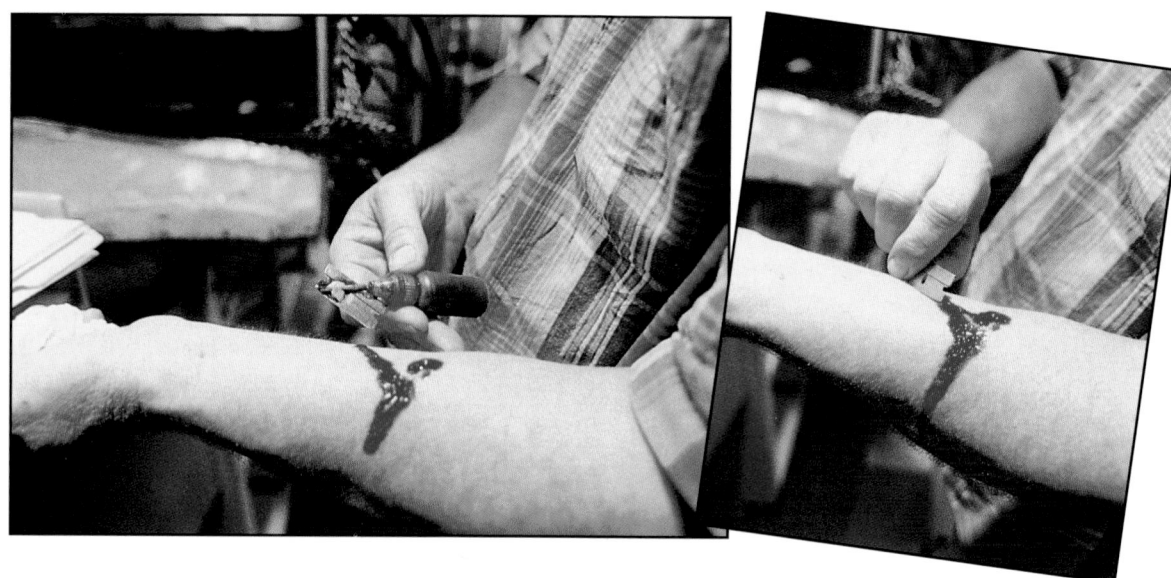

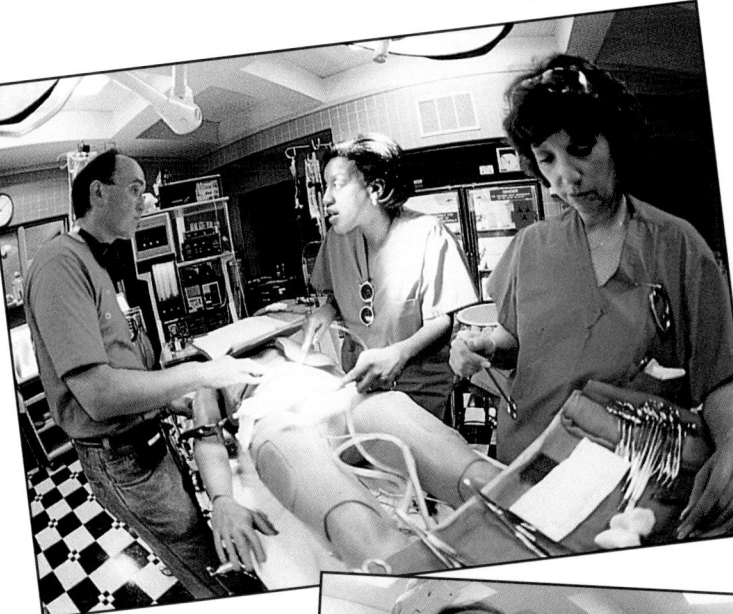

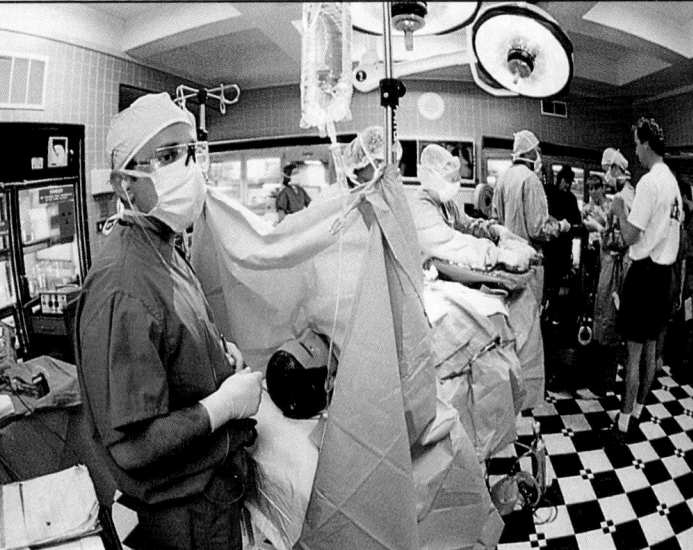

Dr. Sachs, CCH Pounder, and Risa Stefani preparing a dummy patient.

Dr. Sachs displays a manufactured organ.

Dr. Sachs and "patient."

they slipped that intubation tube down the patient's throat. It's a really good display of sleight of hand. They're not just acting—they're like magicians out there."

While the prop crew may use available animal organs from a butcher's shop to approximate real human organs, there are occasions when they need to have items manufactured. There are several prop shops in the Los Angeles area that will simulate whatever organic items are necessary, usually creating them out of silicone, foam, or latex. They will also create silicone characters, such as the injured dog from "Make of Two Hearts" and the newborn infant from "Love's Labor Lost." In the latter episode, an anatomically perfect stunt baby approximating the size and weight of a real newborn was used in 90 percent of the scenes requiring an infant. The makeup department finessed the baby to make it look real and the prop crew added a realistic afterbirth effect made from yogurt and strawberry jam.

The real live babies seen on the show usually come in the form of identical twins or triplets who are allowed to be employed only for limited amounts of time. Whenever a real baby is needed on the set, child

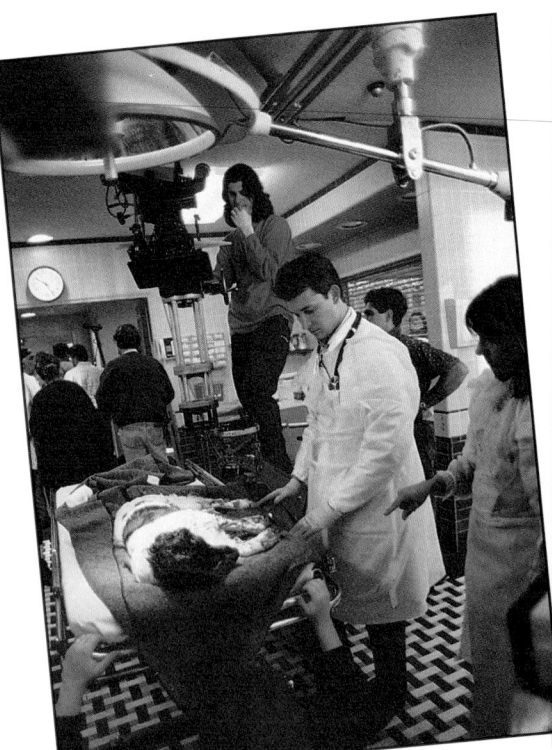

From "Make of Two Hearts," the injured silicone dog.

The proud prop department: Rick Ladomade, Beverly Hadley, Rick Kerns, and baby.

Rick Ladomade at work.

labor laws dictate the presence of a nurse at all times, along with a teacher/welfare worker who makes sure all guidelines for employing children in television and motion pictures are strictly followed. Understandably, the prop department keeps several silicone babies in different sizes to use on stage whenever possible.

For a show with such unusual script requisites as afterbirth, sweat, burns, and scalp lacerations requiring stitches, along with the more pedestrian blood and bruises, the makeup department is an essential part of the *ER* team. The four-person makeup and hair crew is headed up by supervisor "Gandhi Bob" Arrollo, who works with veteran effects makeup artist Werner Keppler. Waldo Sanchez and Rita Bellisimo take care of styling the cast's hair.

Arrollo and Keppler apply makeup on a minimum of sixteen actors each day and oftentimes more depending on the script. They strive to attain a realistic look: some characters are a little overdone, just as they would be in real life; others have a more natural appearance. They keep the principal actors looking as realistic as possible. For characters who are ill, the makeup artists pale down the skin and lips accordingly, and sometimes add dark circles under the eyes. Perspiration is achieved by spritzing on a film of Evian water, avoiding the longer-lasting baby oil and glycerin products that may cause skin or eye irritation. The blood used for injuries is actually made from harmless gels and liquids that are formulated from food extenders. The color of the blood varies as necessary between the blue-red blood from an arterial spurt and the lighter, more commonly used venous blood.

The application of bruises, abrasions, rashes, hives, and melanomas is also part of the everyday routine. "I've done bruises all my life," Arrollo said, laughing. "They're really no big deal. It's just a matter of knowing how old the bruise is. Fresh bruises have a lot of redness because all the capillaries have just been broken. As the bruise gets older, it changes from red to purple to blue and finally to shades of green and yellow as it heals. We basically use different-colored creams and apply them sheerly—depending on the intensity—and then powder them so they don't smear." The

Werner Keppler researching and preparing "burns."

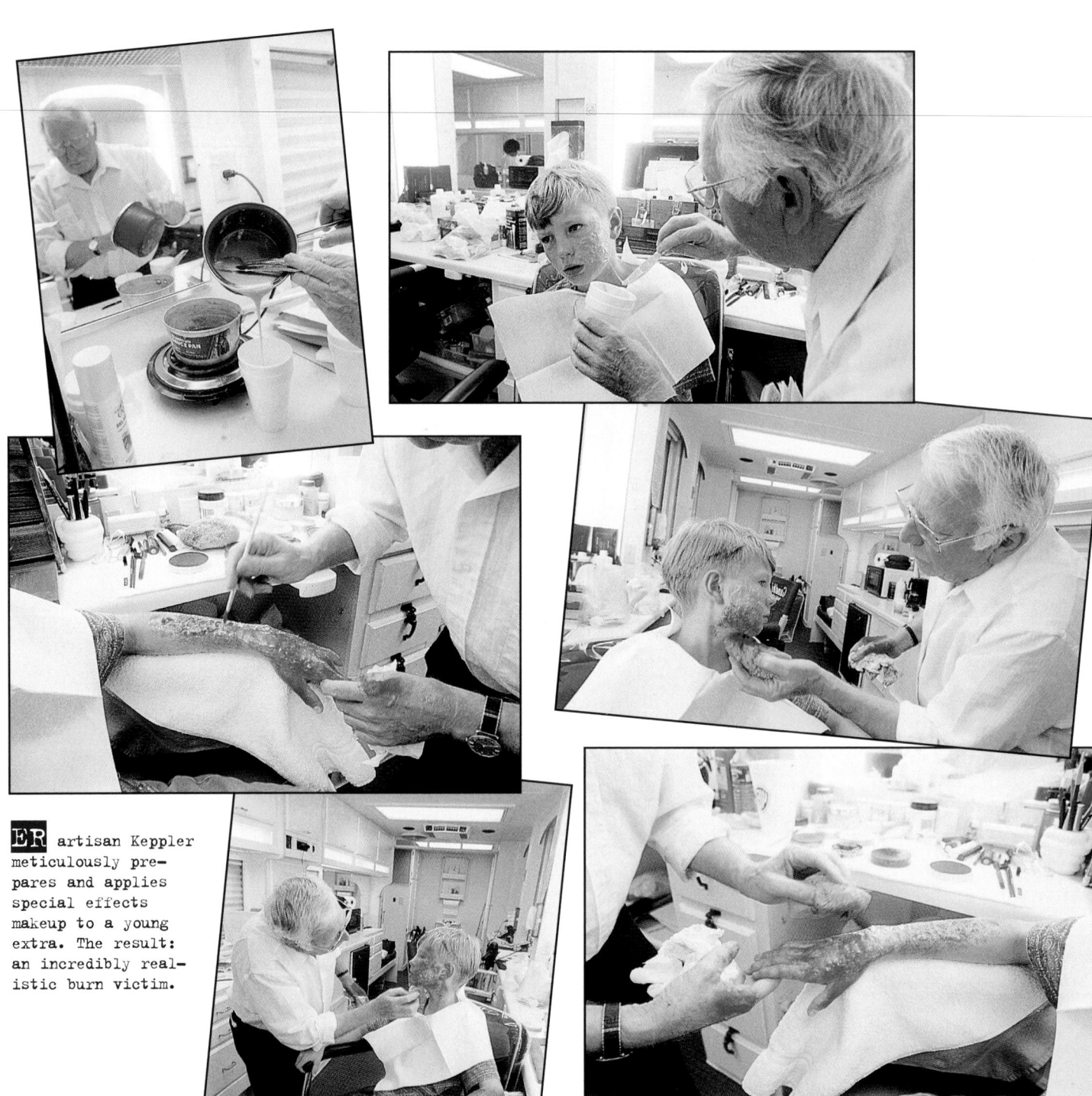

ER artisan Keppler meticulously prepares and applies special effects makeup to a young extra. The result: an incredibly realistic burn victim.

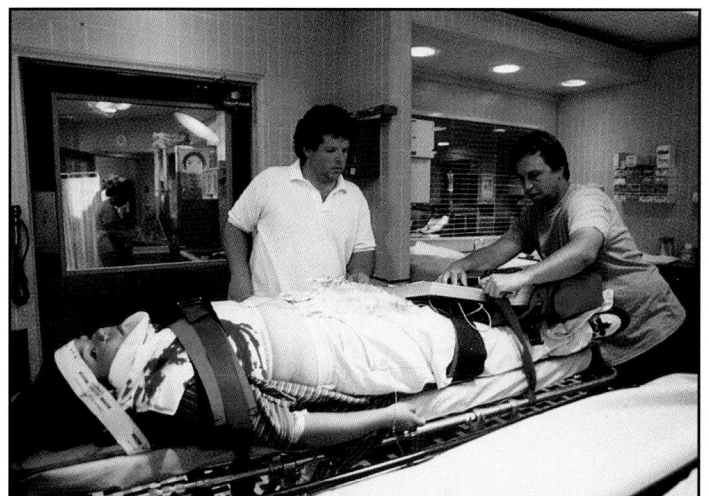

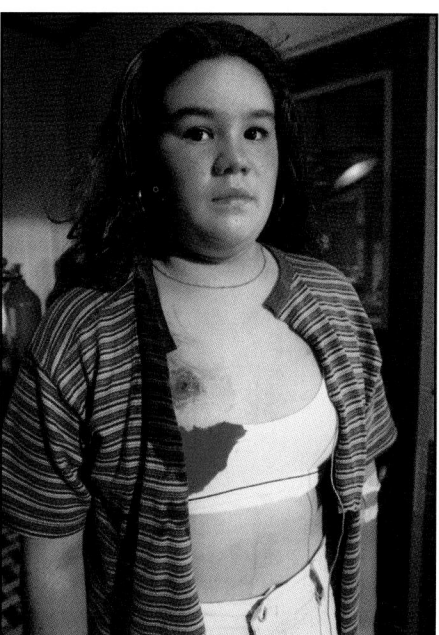

The teamwork of makeup and props provides shockingly true-to-life trauma victims.

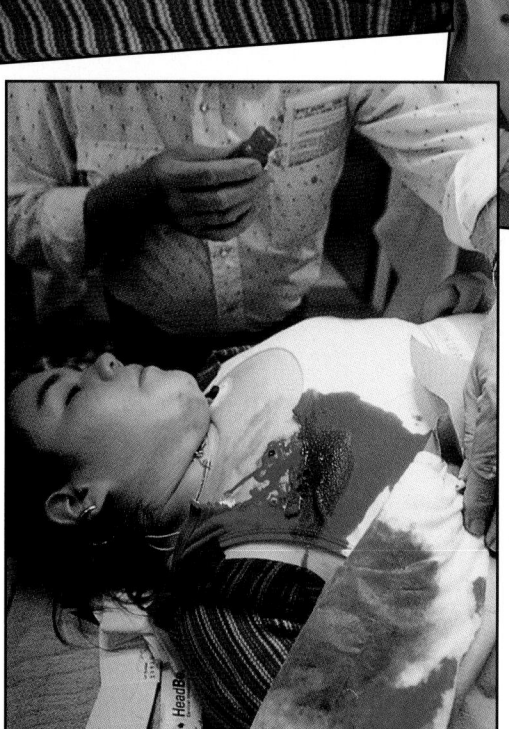

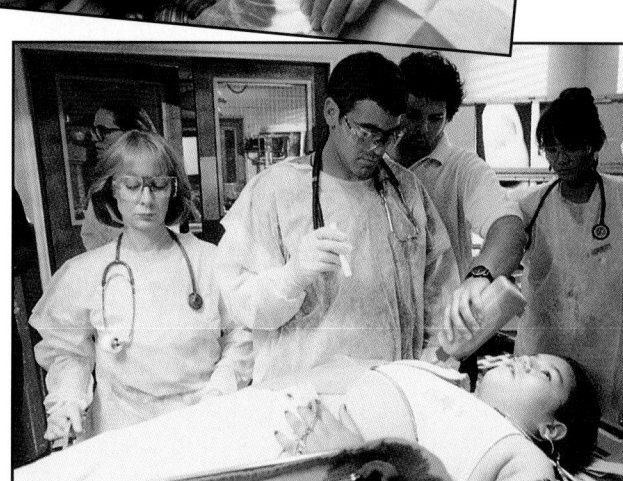

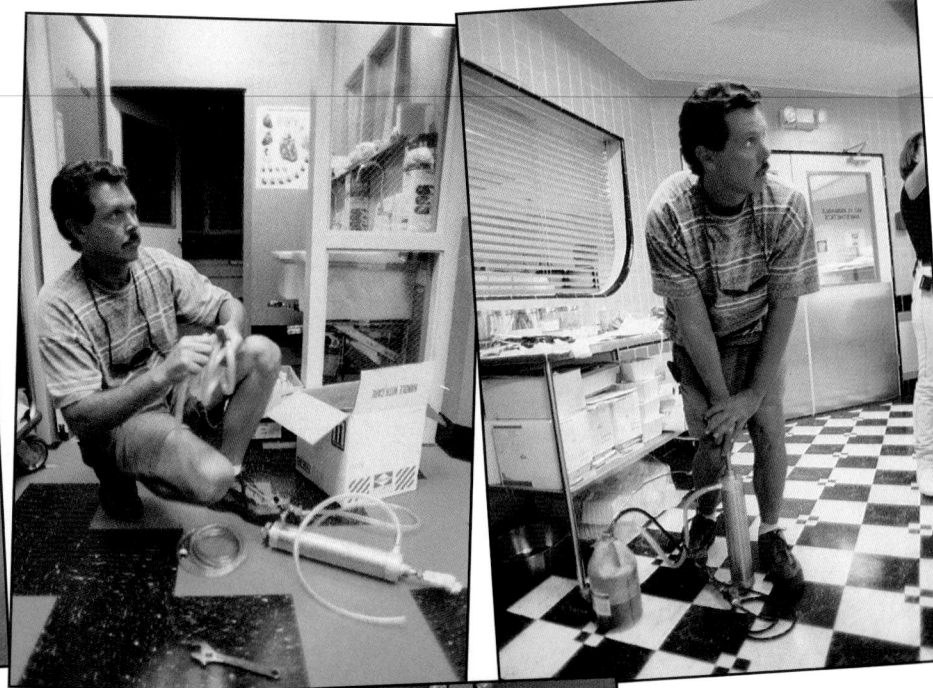

Special effects foreman Scott Forbes rigs a pump and ER table to create "spurting blood."

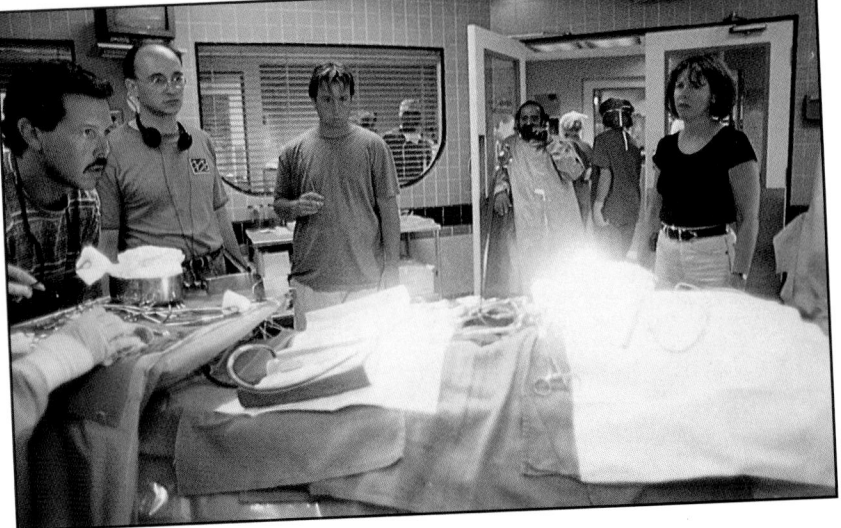

same basic technique is used for other skin injuries and diseases as well. Sachs provides the makeup team with medical books for accurate reference and offers specific first-hand technical advice as needed.

In nearly fifty years as a makeup artist, Keppler has worked on numerous motion pictures and television series, including *Star Trek II: The Wrath of Khan* and all five *Planet of the Apes* films. With this extensive background, he is primarily responsible for preparing the more elaborate makeup effects for the show. Gunshot wounds, knife wounds, and other major traumas involving the application of prosthetic appliances generally fall under his area of expertise. To keep up with the rapid-fire production schedule and the significant number and variety of injuries on a weekly basis, Keppler devised a silicone mold with bullet holes and cuts in an assortment of sizes. Scar-making material—a liquid plastic product that is literally squeezed out of a tube—is added in layers to the molds and then dried, peeled out, and glued onto the actor's skin. The injury is then painted to blend in with the flesh tones, and trauma detail is augmented. Cuts are designed to be raised and slightly open after application, thus permitting on-camera suturing if necessary. The scar material is also a convenient means of applying smaller cuts and open wounds directly to the skin. Burns are achieved by using sheets of special flesh-colored gelatin that are melted down and then cooled and applied to the skin as a liquid. The gelatin is then sculpted and painted to represent disturbingly authentic burns.

Occasionally, more serious trauma effects require additional rigging, and the makeup artists frequently work in collaboration with the prop and special effects departments. For example, a major knife injury to the chest might call for an air bladder and pump causing blood to spurt out. Other injuries might involve meat hooks, chewed ears, or severed limbs. One of Keppler's biggest challenges came with "Love's Labor Lost," when a pregnant abdomen was required for actress Colleen Flynn to wear during the simulated labor and childbirth. Keppler designed the appliance to cover Flynn from neck to upper thigh, with a harness in back for support. The appliance was worn much like a baseball umpire's chest padding, but was perfectly identical to a pregnant woman's torso.

The wizardry of the props department.

With the substantial production elements taken care of and the medical/technical aspects of the scene meticulously orchestrated, the director can then focus on finding the dramatic intent of the story. Leder, for example, approaches the medical scenes just as she would any other: by running the words, finding the meaning of the story, and rehearsing with the actors. With the frenzied pace of television production, however, there is not always as much time for rehearsing as everyone would like. "I try and rehearse with the actors as often as I can," said Leder,

Director Mimi Leder blocks a scene for her actors.

Script supervisor Nancy Karlen (shown with director Felix Alcalà) maintains detailed production and script information, a vital behind-the-scenes reference.

"but with our schedule it's rather hectic. On a feature schedule you'll have weeks of rehearsal. Here we have half an hour. As directors we have to come in very prepared and know exactly what the scene is about so we can discuss it thoroughly with the actors and be ready to shoot on time."

With these extraneous elements in place, Leder then begins to get the scene on its feet. "I decide where the actors are going to walk," she said, "what motivates them to cross from the admitting desk down the hall into a trauma room. After we block it physically, then we fold in the camera. For example, I may want to start out with the camera on Greene's face as he crosses to the admit desk, and then transfer off of Greene's face to Hathaway's and then to Benton's, and then follow Benton down into the trauma room. All that needs to be planned ahead of time."

Once Leder has coordinated the actors and the camera, she adds the background players to the shot, bringing up the camera once again and going through the scene with all the elements at once. "It takes a while to get it going," she said. "It's extremely precisely choreographed, with lots of different layers. To me, it's like dancing. It's storytelling—and it's always the story that leads you where you should point that camera."

On the day of filming, Sachs individually pulls the actors aside for a few minutes, giving them their notes for the scene. "I have to watch these scenes like a hawk," he said, "because I may have, for example, eighteen people doing eighteen different things at once. One person might forget part of his blocking, or someone else may hold an instrument the wrong way. If I catch a mistake during a take, I'll tell the director and the script supervisor and we might be able to make a correction. The frustrating thing for me is that dramatic performance comes before technical

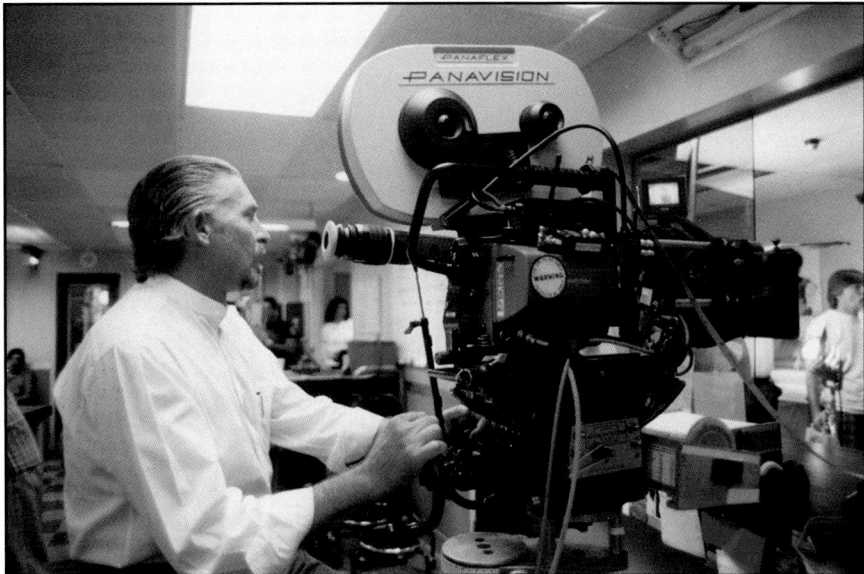

Director of photography Richard Thorpe operating a Panaflex A-camera.

performance. If an actor says a line the way the director and producers love it, but he happens to be holding the forceps incorrectly—of course they are going to use the dramatic moment. We try very, very hard to make sure everything is perfectly accurate, but if we're shooting eight or nine pages a day, we have to get through it quickly and don't have the luxury of really taking our time." Such technical errors rarely make it to the screen, however. Adjustments are made during the editing phase, with a close-up of an actor's face replacing the medical inaccuracy.

Script supervisor Nancy Karlen helps keep the production team on track by carefully logging key information about the production as pertains to the script. For example, Karlin times each scene, notes the size of the lens used, and writes down the shot design and the number of takes. She also makes a note of any dialogue or matching problems. Her records provide an essential reference for the director, the director of photography, the actors, and the postproduction personnel who must later make sense of the multitude of takes and angles shot each day.

Directing a show like *ER* requires creativity and skill at getting the most out of the realistic set. With its maze of hallways and treatment rooms, it provides a multidimensional stage. As such, the camera on *ER* is not a stationary tool aimed in one or two directions for scene after scene. It is as much a part of the storytelling process as the actors, props, and scenery. *ER* episode directors collaborate closely with director of photography Richard Thorpe in getting the most out of *ER*'s lighting and camera equipment—a standard Panaflex A-camera (main camera) and a Panaflex Steadicam—and in the technical composition of the shots. Both the A-camera and the Steadicam are operated by Guy Norman Bee.

Some of the more lengthy sequences are shot in one long, continuous take without editorial cuts interrupting the flow of the image. Such shots are called "one-ers" and are typically, though not always, filmed with the Steadicam. The Steadicam is also used for trauma scenes and other instances where protracted and very active takes are called for. All told, about 70 percent of the shots on *ER* are achieved with the Steadicam.

The Steadicam is equipped with a special spring-loaded rigging

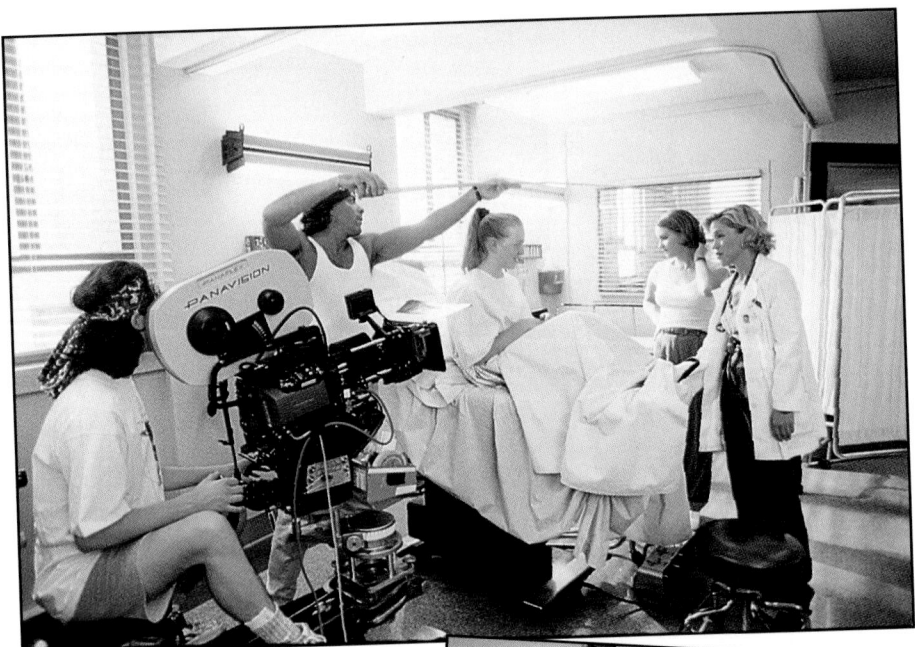

Guy Norman Bee operating an A-camera and the Steadicam.

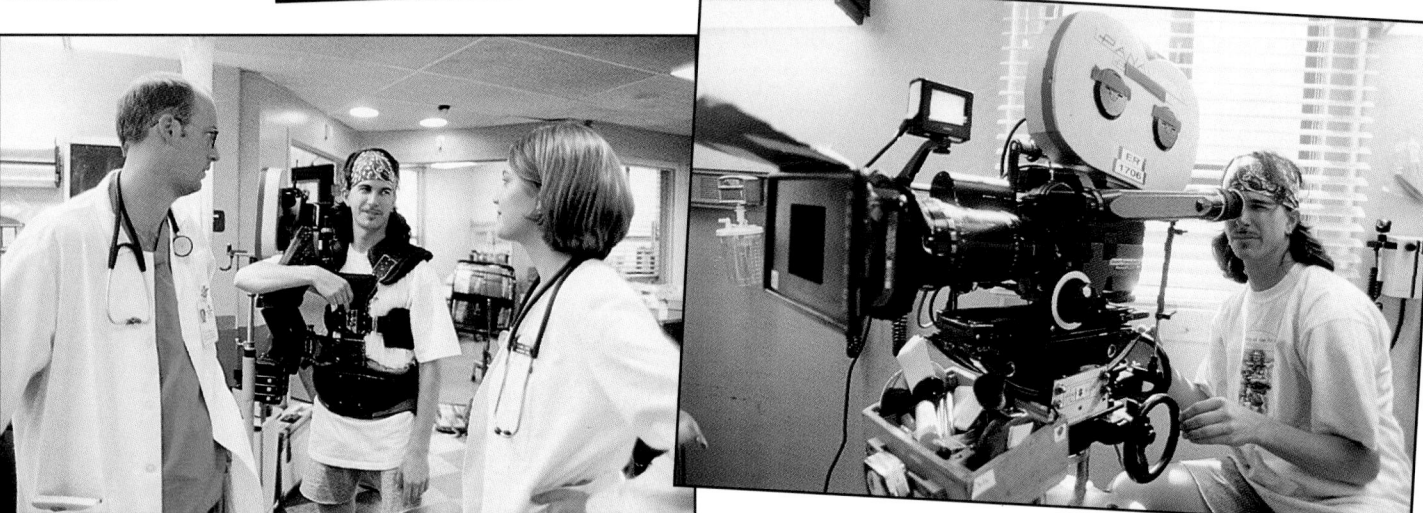

that combines the freedom of a handheld camera with the stability of a dollied tracking shot. This creates the smooth, flowing appearance of the shot as the cameraman walks along. Although the weight is considerable at seventy pounds, it is reasonably distributed by way of a harness onto the hips of the cameraman. Instead of an eyepiece, the scene is viewed through a five-inch video monitor.

"There are a lot of things to worry about while operating the Steadicam," said Bee. "First of all, 'assassins' can show up in the frame that will ruin a shot—microphones or reflections in the glass that shouldn't be there. I always carry a lot of black T-shirts so that if I have to pass by a piece of glass, I hopefully become invisible. Plus, I have to navigate as I walk. I have to go through sets and doorways and halls and back up very quickly—without running into anyone or anything. And I don't use a spotter because it's just another person I can get tangled up with. I also have to think about composition, and make sure the director is getting what he or she wants. Actually, my goal is to give the directors more than they ever bargained for."

"The Steadicam lends a verité sort of feeling to the show," Thorpe noted. "We want the camera to be, not a participant, but a very close observer of all the action—and to bring the audience in so that they become close observers as well. In that sense, there are no real tricks going on with the camera work on *ER*. We just keep the camera very, very close to what's going on, and keep the energy and movement in each shot."

Despite the kinetic, fast-moving style of the show, Leder understands the importance of pausing for moments of tenderness or reflection. "One of the things I find interesting about *ER* is that it's nonstop movement and emotion—and then everything stops and we take a moment and we see a man kiss his dead wife and say good-bye to her. Or we come to a waiting room full of Polish people singing and dancing, because they just came from a wedding and they're waiting for all their relatives who have food poisoning. There's a lot of juxtaposition in the storytelling that is very visual and visceral emotionally. I think that's an important element of the show."

Although the pilot for ER remained true to Crichton's original concept and established its trademark style and turbulent pace, the series has evolved and grown since then. "I feel the style of the show actually looks quite different from the pilot," said Leder. "The pilot probably had about twenty percent Steadicam and a lot of hard cutting. Obviously, we use more Steadicam and there are some other differences in interpretation. But Rod Holcomb really set the tone in the pilot, which was a springboard for us to take off from. We were able to take the magnificent world that Michael Crichton created and explore that world and find it in our own way. We hope that this show will have many more years to explore."

On the Set
Warner Bros. Studios, Burbank
August 7, 1995

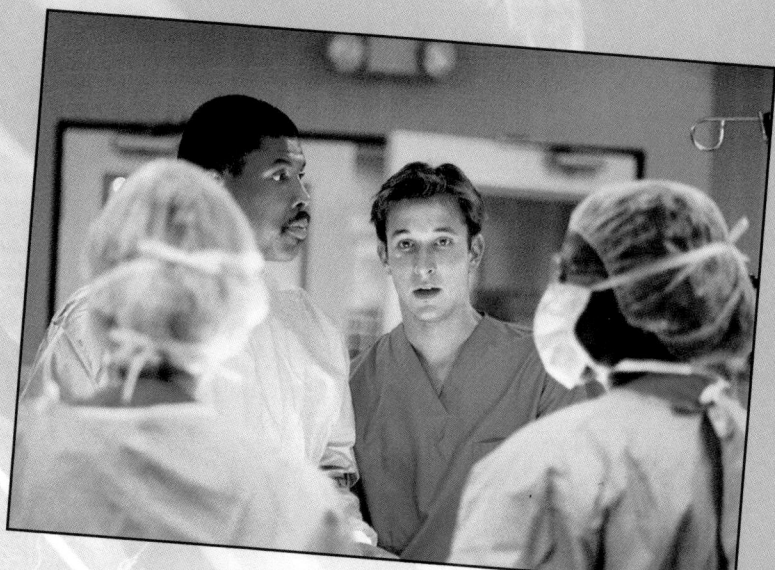

The video monitor is set up in a treatment room—down the stairwell and across two hallways from the erratic black-and-white image it is receiving. Mimi Leder sits in her director's chair watching the screen without concern. This morning's shoot has gone very well, and she knows Steadicam operator Guy Bee will soon have the shot framed to her satisfaction. Besides that, she is surrounded by Richard Thorpe, Chris Chulack, and Joe Sachs, who are teasing her about taking the afternoon off. Leder takes it good-naturedly; it has just been announced that she has received an Emmy nomination for her direction of "Love's Labor Lost" and there is a spirit of celebration in the air.

The video screen becomes steady and the production team is immediately attentive. Bee is ready at the top of the stairs. His Steadicam is focused so tightly on the backs of Eriq La Salle and Noah Wyle that the picture looks black at first. Leder shouts, "Action!" and the actors walk down the stairs with Bee close behind. From the treatment room vantage point, the camera seems to float after them like an invisible eye. Bee and the actors navigate a surprisingly sharp corner, walk past the elevator, and meet up with Julianna Margulies, who heads off in another direction. Bee picks up her action and follows her down a different corridor.

Bee's movement is fluid and graceful. He wears the seventy pounds of camera and harness as if they were nothing. He has walked the rooms and hallways of the *ER* set on countless occasions and knows their curves and angles by heart. He never knows, however, when he might get bumped by one of the many crossing extras or when a microphone will accidentally

dip into frame. As Bee nearly finishes his course, the camera is abruptly jarred and the shot is spoiled. Leder takes it in stride. With the Steadicam such an integral part of the show, the bump is the equivalent of an actor dropping his line.

Bee and the actors return to the top of the stairs and the background players are reset. They walk the course several times more, with each subsequent take growing stronger and more eloquent. "Operating the Steadicam takes a massive amount of practice and knowing what good composition is," said Bee. "It's kind of hard to define, almost like a musician having a natural ear. He knows when it sounds good, when it has the right amount of vibrato, tone, attack. It's the same thing with a good Steadicam shot. A lot goes into the composition and timing—and sometimes into finding different ways of looking at things."

Leder's eyes are glued to the monitor. The shot is crying out for a "wipe"—an actor crossing abruptly in front of the camera at the last minute—to bring it to a close. To the casual observer, the scene looks fine as it is. The camera moves have been perfected, the actors' lines are down pat, and the urgency of the moment is beautifully conveyed. On the next take, however, the wipe is added for punctuation and the effect is clearly different. Leder, as it turns out, was right.

Chapter 4
Chicago

The producers of *ER* have to look no further than real life for inspiration. The walls of their hospital sets are lined with authentic Sharps biohazard infectious waste containers and tattered health posters that advise against smoking. On cue, real-life nurses pass intubation trays straight out of a medical supply catalogue. Characters sort through personal issues with as much clarity—or as little—as the audience that watches week by week, and high-intensity trauma is played against the anticlimax of a coffee break. A hundred invisible elements of reality resonate through the sounds and images on every episode of *ER*.

The producers are well aware that realism is made up of countless such large and small components. Because of this, they take the show to Chicago several times each year to capture the reality of a location that cannot be duplicated any other place—while at the same time creating a perfect contrast to the insular world of the ER. "All our interiors are four-wall sets with hard ceilings," John Wells noted, "just like a real emergency room, which is partly why *ER* seems like a documentary in some ways. There's a claustrophobic feeling in the hospital that contributes to the visual style of the show. So when we go outside of the hospital, we want it to be big and open. We want the audience to have the sense that these people are in a pressure cooker at work, that their medical lives happen in this crowded interior, and that their personal lives are out in the big open spaces of Chicago. This creates two very different contrasting visual styles."

Exterior footage of Chicago provides one other essential element of realism: the city itself. There is no place like Chicago but Chicago, and

On location in Chicago, under the El, Mimi Leder directs Noah Wyle.

beyond the rich architecture and well-known landmarks, there are certain locations that have become specific to the show. During the first season and the beginning of the second, for example, the entrance to the emergency room of the University of Illinois at Chicago Hospital doubled for the exterior of *ER*'s County General. For these shots, the outside wall of the hospital was dressed with a blue County General Hospital sign and stunt ambulances and police cars were rented as necessary. Near the emergency entrance is an El track, which was frequently featured in shots as trains roared past. Shooting here was highly effective, but troublesome at times. Because UIC has a working emergency room, the facility could not shut down or reroute patients for the convenience of the show. When real patient-bearing ambulances arrived at the door, the production company immediately and respectfully stopped working and cleared the way for the genuine emergency to be handled. Additionally, the writers and producers felt the need to take the story immediately outside the hospital more frequently than the trips to Chicago permitted. New exteriors built on the Warner Bros. back lot allowed the production company to capture the hospital exteriors more conveniently, and made it possible to spend more of the Chicago time at locations that were less easily duplicated.

The roof of the Chicago Fire Department Academy is another key location. It serves as the hospital's emergency helicopter landing pad, and is featured whenever such emergencies are dictated by the script. The Fire Academy rooftop was chosen because of its standing as an FAA registered helicopter landing site and its close proximity to downtown Chicago, which revealed much of the familiar skyline as a backdrop. Whenever emergency helicopter landing shots are planned, *ER* works in cooperation with Dr. Ira J. Blumen, who is the program/medical director for the University of Chicago Aeromedical Network and serves as one of *ER*'s Chicago-based medical/technical advisers.

ER travels to Chicago three or four times each season to spend several highly organized days shooting the locations that will be featured throughout several of the upcoming episodes. All logistical issues are facilitated by Chicago unit production manager and location director of photography Robert Hudisek of RAH Producers Center. In preparation for the location shoot, Christopher Chulack sends Hudisek pages from the script called "temporary first-page runs" indicating the intent of the scenes and giving Hudisek a good idea of what will be needed. "We break the pages down according to what each scene may need," said Hudisek, "whether it's four dogs, fifty possible extras, or a police car.

Leder, Wyle, and Margulies.

On-location filming requires special additional professionals: actors, prop and costume people, and others.

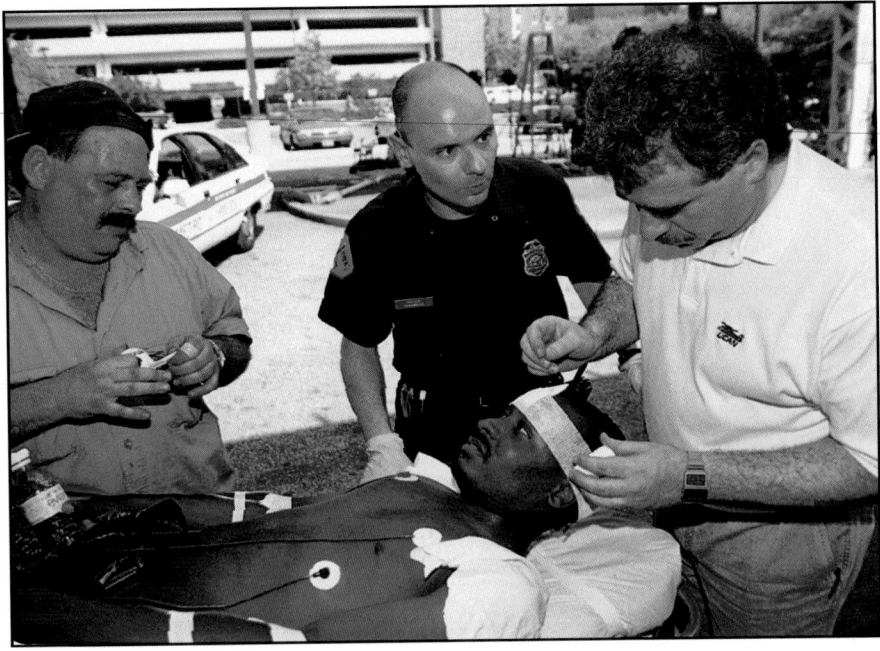

From this we come up with a one-line schedule of what it would take to shoot these elements."

At this point, no locations have been determined by either the script or the production company. Hudisek, however, reads the temporary pages with a practiced eye. "Thoughts come to mind. I'll think, well, if I did shoot this here, the way it's described, we could possibly do it on Wednesday or Thursday—or, they won't let us use this location until a Saturday. Things tend to fall into place." Hudisek also considers locations from two different perspectives: fundamental practicality and cinematic aesthetics. "We have to consider whether or not we can get all the equipment in and out of a location. For example, if a fourth-floor walk-up is called for in the script, we have to think about the hours it would take to get all the equipment up and down. A first-floor apartment might work just as well, as long as we don't need to see anything through the windows. As a cinematographer, I am aware of the direction of the sun and sight lines and can plan for a location accordingly. Our job is to be as efficient as possible and create the best product on the screen for the least cost factor."

By the time the Los Angeles team is nearly ready to arrive, the first revisions of the script—indicating changes and deletions—have usually been determined. Hudisek and crew then come up with a working schedule factoring in the sites, the number of additional elements called for in the script, and the amount of time available. As soon as he gets the okay from Warner Bros., Hudisek and location manager Karyn McCarthy begin scouting possible sites and making final arrangements for the shoot. They work in cooperation with the Chicago Film Office and the Illinois Film Office to obtain whatever general permits are necessary.

While locations are being firmed up, Hudisek begins to mobilize the army of production personnel and the accompanying lighting, sound, and camera equipment essential to the shoot. Transportation is meticulously coordinated under the supervision of Dick D'Angelo; props are readied by prop master Bob Volpe; and hair, makeup, and costume crews are alerted and begin to prepare their departments. Chicago-based guest stars and extras are quickly booked for the shoot, and the problems of providing food and drinks for nearly ninety people each day are solved by the craft services department. Within six days after receiving the go-ahead from Warner's, the Chicago team is in final pre-production. By the seventh day, the L.A. cast and crew members have arrived and begun filming.

Location shooting is scheduled to take advantage of the weather and distinctive seasons, but doesn't always coincide with the intensive pace of the *ER* writing process. Oftentimes scripts are only partially completed prior to departure for Chicago. For example, scenes for the first four episodes of the second season were filmed during a concentrated three-day shoot in July 1995. The directors responsible for those episodes—Mimi Leder, Eric Laneuville, and Felix Alcalà—were on hand to direct exterior segments that would be cut into shows scheduled for filming weeks later. Also present were

Director Felix Alcalà, Tommy Burns, and Chicago unit production manager Robert Hudisek.

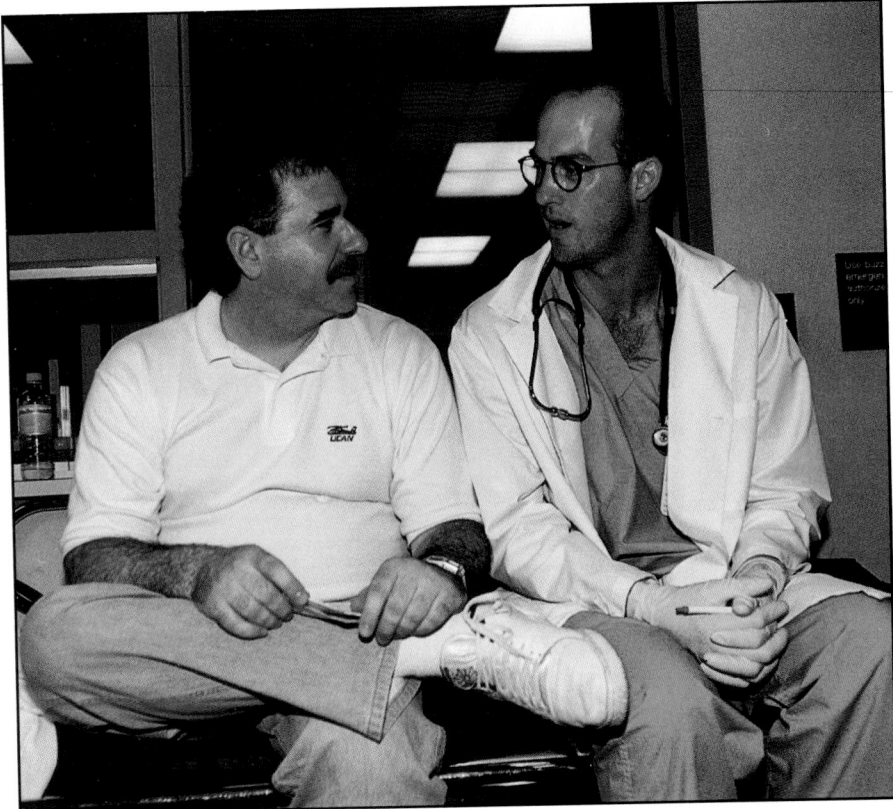

two of the writer/producers for *ER*: Paul Manning, who wrote the third episode, and Carol Flint, who wrote the fourth. John Wells remained in Los Angeles, where he finished writing Episode 1, as did Lydia Woodward, who was busy completing the script for the second show.

As with Wells and Woodward, Manning and Flint had just partially completed their scripts. Of necessity, they had finalized only the scenes that demanded immediate completion for the purposes of location filming. The story lines had been thoroughly worked through at writers meetings by this point, but outlines for the episodes had evolved into rough drafts at best. Finalized scripts were still several weeks away. The writers' presence in Chicago was vital to the actors, who had yet to see *any* writing and needed to understand the arcs their characters had taken during the lengthy summertime writers meetings that had taken place back at Warner Bros. during their hiatus.

"It's very tough for the actors to perform when they haven't seen a script," said Manning. "It's also very difficult for us to write scenes that are separate from the script as a whole. As writers, we talked through the beats of what precedes the various scenes, of course, but in the case of Episode 3, I had to write a location scene for Benton and Jeanie—and not a single scene had been written for them since the previous season.

We talked through where they *should* be, but talking doesn't give you the nuances. In this case, the first go at the material just didn't click. I rewrote it the morning before we shot it in a totally different way. It's all trial and error really, and it is very easy to make a mistake. You hope you get it right, but it's a matter of figuring out where the characters should be and using your imagination as to what's gone before."

Beyond keeping all the story lines straight and generating just the right dialogue to propel that story, producers Manning and Flint are haunted by practical considerations as well. "When you're a producer as well as a writer," said Flint, "you have to make yourself forget what you know about production limitations. You have to stop yourself from thinking, 'Oh my God, how are we ever going to hold the traffic on Michigan Avenue!' and just write the story. We write the scenes for Chicago knowing they get winnowed down out of necessity; we just don't like to think about it while we're doing it. That's the good thing about having four or five different people writing scenes. Everybody can write with a full commitment and know that Chris Chulack and Mimi Leder will deal with the practicalities and cut whatever isn't going to fit into the schedule."

Given the conflict between the desired number of shots and the practical limitations of time and money, it is sometimes necessary to adjust the actual number of shots. Ultimately, however, enough footage is gathered to suit the needs of the story. "A lot of television

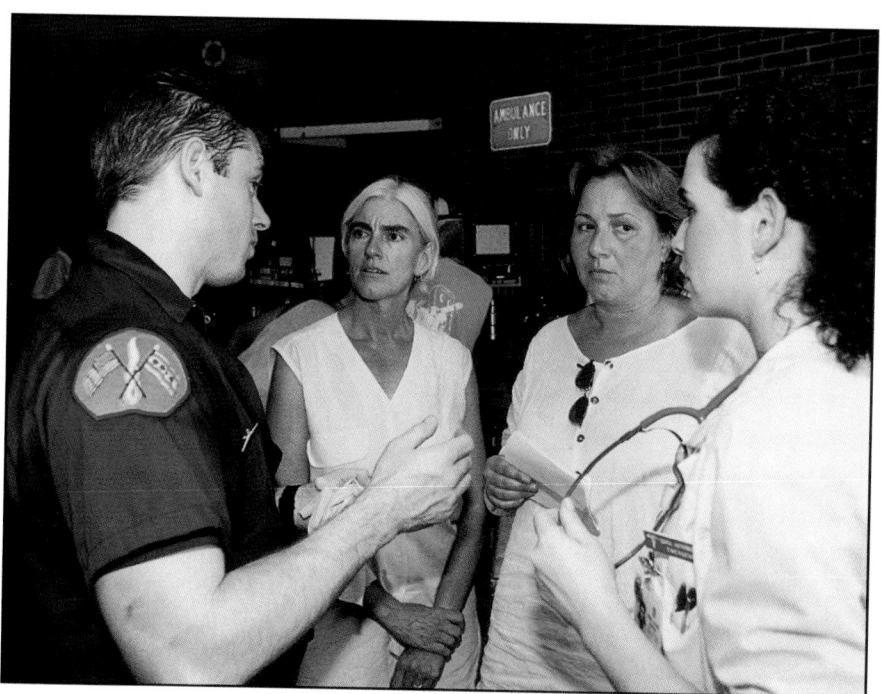

Writer-producer Carol Flint and director Mimi Leder flanked by Ron Eldard and Julianna Margulies.

production is compromise," said Flint, "and really good producers, people like Chris and Mimi, know how to make those compromises without sacrificing quality. They can make hard choices about what to lose and what to save while still holding on to what the story is really about."

By the end of each location shoot, *ER* has collected enough footage of Chicago to blend seamlessly with the interior dramas played out on sound stages nearly two thousand miles away.

ON THE SET
UNIVERSITY OF ILLINOIS HOSPITAL, CHICAGO
JULY 14, 1995

The light in Chicago is unlike the light in other places. Its clear white quality, born of a northern latitude, cannot be easily duplicated in the golden haze of Southern California. Neither can the city's familiar landmarks. The elevated train, known as the El, is uniquely its own. So are Navy Pier, the Chicago River, and Michigan Avenue. Chicago itself generates a vibration that eludes easy analysis.

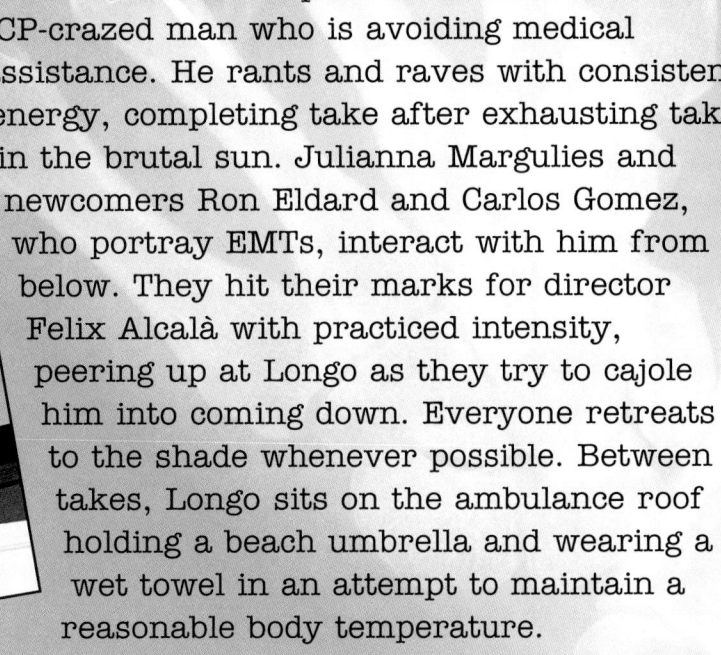

This stifling July morning finds the *ER* company encamped outside the University of Illinois at Chicago Hospital emergency entrance, where they are filming scenes from Episode 3. Actor Tony Longo, a powerfully built former football player, strides across the top of an ambulance as a PCP-crazed man who is avoiding medical assistance. He rants and raves with consistent energy, completing take after exhausting take in the brutal sun. Julianna Margulies and newcomers Ron Eldard and Carlos Gomez, who portray EMTs, interact with him from below. They hit their marks for director Felix Alcalà with practiced intensity, peering up at Longo as they try to cajole him into coming down. Everyone retreats to the shade whenever possible. Between takes, Longo sits on the ambulance roof holding a beach umbrella and wearing a wet towel in an attempt to maintain a reasonable body temperature.

The heat was even worse yesterday. *ER*'s first day of location shooting was marked by the highest recorded temperature in Chicago's history. Engulfed by high midwestern humidity and one-hundred-six-degree heat, the production company sweltered in downtown locations on Michigan Avenue and Wacker Drive, where Mimi Leder shot segments with Eriq La Salle and Noah Wyle for the second season's premiere episode.

The company finished the day at Navy Pier—a lengthy promenade extending along Lake Michigan and bearing an assortment of vendors, entertainment venues, and a five-story Ferris wheel. Under the direction of Eric Laneuville, scenes for Episode 2 were captured under a late-afternoon sun that was as unrelenting as it had been that morning.

At least there is shade available today. The El track that rises above the emergency room entrance casts a shadow that lowers the temperature a few degrees. Trains roar by in north- and southbound increments and are timed by a spotter to flash across camera on cue. First assistant director Tommy Burns listens to his walkie-talkie and shouts, "A minute and a half!" The actors quickly take their places and prepare to act against the deafening backdrop. Alcalà gets his shot and the crew readjusts the equipment for another, quieter setup.

It is nearly time to break for lunch when the scene's conclusion is shot. A syringe is prepared for Eldard to jab into Longo's carefully padded backside. The sequence is shot several times with varying degrees of success. Either the syringe hangs limply and falls out, or Eldard has trouble getting it to puncture Longo's padding. On two occasions, the needle misses the padding altogether and sticks Longo instead. Whatever happens, the actor stays perfectly in character and completes the take without missing a beat.

Alcalà finally gives the call for lunch and the company retreats into the cool interior of a hospital conference room to eat and recover for an hour. They will return to work under the direction of Leder and film the rest of the afternoon at the hospital before packing up camp and moving to another location in the final hours of dusk.

Chapter 5
The Actors

Anthony Edwards / "Dr. Mark Greene"

When actor Anthony Edwards first became involved with *ER*, he knew it would be interesting to find out how his character—whom he thought of as "St. Mark"—would fall from grace. "Mark Greene could really do no wrong at first," said Edwards. "He was great with patients, he had good camaraderie with people, and he was even-tempered. And I knew, because of the way the series was set up, that the fun was going to be in finding out where he trips and falls, what makes him upset, and what really means something to him. It's been interesting to learn about him as the scripts have evolved."

As it turned out, Greene ended up grappling with issues far removed from the easy life of sainthood. The second season offered even greater challenges. "Greene faced a lot of changes in dealing with the new responsibilities of becoming an attending physician," said Edwards. "There are more politics involved than when he was chief resident, which means that he can no longer practice pure medicine. He's faced with becoming an administrator, and I think that's hard for him. Greene's relationship with his wife is troublesome, too. He has a fear of intimacy, and now that his marriage is in crisis, a lot is required of him that he didn't expect; things are out of control. I think he has problems in his interpersonal relationships and, like a lot of people, he hides behind his work."

As with all the characters on *ER*, the path to

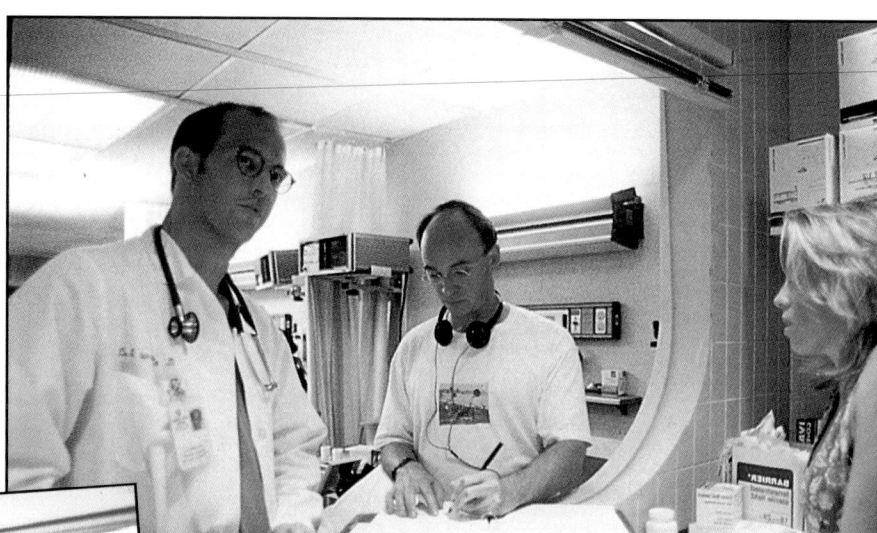

understanding Greene can be found in the writing. Edwards sees it as the most fundamental route. "The writing is the basic foundation and the complete blueprint, map, and resource you have to fall back on. You can always go back to the script to find the information you need. If it's not there, maybe you weren't looking hard enough. Writing and acting are totally different processes. In fact, it's not great for actors to be involved in the writers' process because an actor's job is more about interpreting the writing and then trying to bring some new dimension to it. An actor's work isn't about creating something from scratch. If you create from scratch, you're missing out on the collaboration between the writers—or the work of one particular writer for that episode. And their imagination is far better in that arena than mine will ever be as an actor." With road map in hand, acting then becomes a journey of discovery. "Acting is a process of revealing things about yourself all the time—no matter who the character is. Any character you play requires something different from your experience. The job of acting is to find those places where your fears live or your love lives or your passion or your curiosity."

Audience perception also shades the way a character is defined. "I think actors have different images of characters," said Edwards, "and so do audiences. To some people, Mark Greene was never a saint because he wasn't a great father or a great husband. They didn't even care about the medicine—they just saw Greene as someone who had a tremendous number of character faults. So, as an actor, you never want to judge a character, you just want to play him. You want to be as honest and as spontaneous as you can. The characters all change in relation to other characters anyway. Drama's all about conflict, and conflict comes from you wanting one thing and the other person wanting something else."

Trusting the audience to be thinking participants in the storytelling process has been part of the *ER* fabric from the show's inception. "Michael Crichton was very clear from the beginning that it was important not to oversentimentalize or overdo things on *ER* because that's not how it happens in life," said Edwards. "Sometimes things go by and you feel them later. We're trying to let the audience be the fly on the wall. They're not spoon-fed or told how to feel. A lot of that is to John Wells's credit; he makes a point of never condescending to the audience. The philosophy is you don't treat them like children and they don't watch it like children—they pay attention to the story because they want to. There's a very destructive myth that audiences are stupid. Well, you reap whatever you sow. People watch television for entertainment, and if they're entertained in a full way for forty-five or fifty minutes, the experience can be very rich. They can be scared and amused and challenged and taken on a journey that's complete."

ER's triumph as a dramatic series was immediate and enduring—and a phenomenon that took nearly everyone by surprise. "For a long time we were saying that the show's success is something undefinable," said Edwards, "but I think it *is* definable. I think it comes from having writers, producers, directors, actors, technicians, designers, and editors working to their best ability and being supported in doing that. If filmmaking is a collaborative art form, that's what's going on here. Everybody gets spurred on by everybody else doing well, and that keeps the level high and the expectation high. You don't want to let your end down. So, besides it being good timing and a story that people want to get into, I think we do it well. On all levels. And we all feel a great sense of pride.

"People have certain perceptions about what makes a drama or what makes a sitcom. But good sitcoms have great dramas in them, and the best dramas have a lot of lightness and comedy to them. It's always been that way. You only limit yourself by giving yourself limitations. When Josh Brand won the Emmy for *Northern Exposure* he said, 'In television, the

only limitations are that you can't swear and you can't be naked.' Now, even that's going away a bit. And so, as audiences, people should demand quality. It's only laziness that creates inane television. People want to say, 'What's the formula? What's the rule?' There is none, and that's the thing you have to embrace. You're responsible for creating your own."

George Clooney / "Dr. Douglas Ross"

In the pilot, Dr. Doug Ross arrives at the hospital first thing in the morning after an all-night binge. He is charming and engaging, but his problem with alcohol is clearly apparent. He also turns out to be something of a womanizer; a man accustomed to his good looks and easy manner taking him wherever he wants to go. Then later, almost quietly, Ross surprises us with his tenderness toward his young patients. He is a compassionate pediatrician who looks into their eyes with empathy and seems to have an uncanny understanding of pain. When he turns with fury on the parents who may be abusing these children, we can't help but cheer.

Actor George Clooney's character is described in one episode as "a reasonably normal guy with sloppy impulse control." The assessment seems fairly accurate. "Doug Ross is a guy in his mid-thirties," said Clooney, "who has just discovered that all the things he used to do in life—partying a little too hard and chasing girls a little too

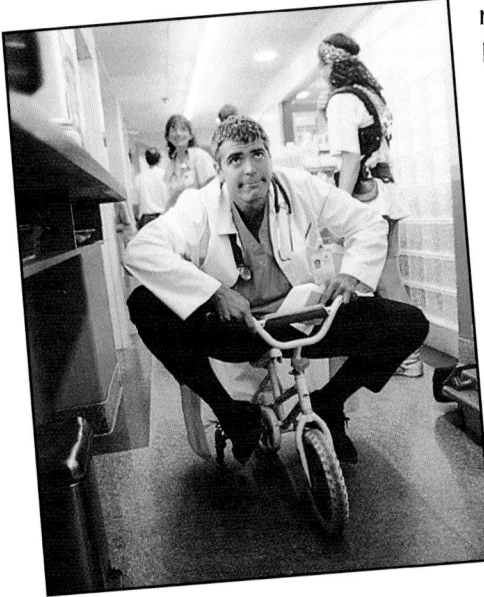

much—are all starting to catch up to him. It's not working like it used to. He is faced with having to deal with his inadequacies as an adult."

Like the other characters on the show, Ross is fallible—an attribute the audience seems to accept without reservation. "John Wells has made the characters important," noted Clooney, "because he understands that the audience relates to the story through the characters. The directors contribute in the same way. For instance, the Hathaway-Ross love scenario wasn't really in the pilot script at all; Rod Holcomb created it simply by using camera angles. Her suicide attempt became personal because the audience saw it through Ross's eyes. The same thing happened with the childbirth scene. You watched it through Noah Wyle's eyes, as Carter, the new boy on the set. The writers do a brilliant job with the script, and the directors make it even better."

With the vigorous *ER* production pace, it is sometimes difficult for the actors to indulge in the luxury of personal exploration as they define their characters. Of necessity, Clooney's approach is very straightforward. "Whatever method you choose to work with is fine. Brando would have been great had he *not* been a 'method' actor.

Actors are good or not good based on their individual talent. If you are in a play or a good film, you can piece together a performance based on personal history and other elements that add color to the character. On *ER*, we show up every morning and have as many as nine pages to shoot. Some of it's about the character, and some of it's a matter of survival. So what you learn to do is tell yourself a story. What is really going on in this scene? What am I trying to do? And you just do it very quickly; it becomes second nature to you. There is a danger of it getting too comfortable after a while and you may have to shake things up, but in general it's a much quicker process than it would be under other circumstances.

"I've done a lot of bad television over the years—and I've been very bad in a lot of bad television—so I have a pretty good perspective of what we do on *ER*. We are on a tremendous television show. And I will hold what we do against any actor's job as far as difficulty goes; doing a play for eight performances a week is nothing compared to this. Every single workday is fourteen or fifteen hours long. We speak a language we don't understand; nobody comes to work in the morning knowing what 'tachycardia' means. We have to perform medical procedures as if we were professionals—and we have to do that with fifty extras flying through on a Steadicam shot with no cuts, saying, 'Super ventricular tachyarrhythmia'—without screwing up. It's an ongoing all-day process, and it takes great concentration."

Sherry Stringfield / "Dr. Susan Lewis"

Actress Sherry Stringfield can sum up her character with a quote from the pilot. It happens during a scene where Dr. Susan Lewis is treating a man who *seems* to be in the advanced stages of lung cancer; his X rays, combined with a history of coughing blood and weight loss, point clearly in that direction. Without more conclusive testing, however, Lewis is unwilling to commit to a diagnosis. The patient presses her until she relents: how long does he have to live? Six months to a year. It is at this moment that Lewis reveals her fundamental philosophy when she tells him, ". . . Nothing is certain. Nothing that seems very bad and nothing that seems very good. Nothing is certain. Nothing."

For Stringfield, this seems to say it all.

Her character, the pragmatic Dr. Susan Lewis, rolls with the punches in much the same way. "I like Lewis because she always seems to do things to the best of her ability—whether she realizes it or not. She's very thorough in her life, especially as a doctor. She sees a situation, she

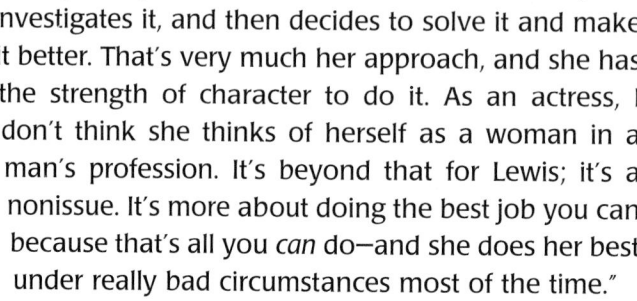

investigates it, and then decides to solve it and make it better. That's very much her approach, and she has the strength of character to do it. As an actress, I don't think she thinks of herself as a woman in a man's profession. It's beyond that for Lewis; it's a nonissue. It's more about doing the best job you can because that's all you *can* do—and she does her best under really bad circumstances most of the time."

With a sister like Chloe and a mother like Cookie (who appeared in the "Motherhood" episode only to tell Lewis that it was just too difficult for her to help out with the new baby) it's easy to understand the character's inherent problem-solving skills. "It must have been a horror show for Lewis," said Stringfield, "but it helps explain her growth as a character. Over the course of the first season she really gained a lot of confidence. She learned to stand up for herself and her patient. I think she began to understand how to utilize the hospital rules and the bureaucracy much better than before. She seemed to realize, 'I *do* know what I'm doing, you guys deal with it.' "

Stringfield approached her role as an authority figure in the same matter-of-fact way. "I did a lot of research about the medical profession in the beginning. There couldn't be even a flash of doubt about what I was doing. I wanted to understand every single word. I wanted to know why one treatment would be ordered instead of another. Once I learned those things, however, I realized that it all had to be second nature. The medical dialogue had to be comparable to me saying, 'Go to the store and get some pita bread, some hummus, and flowers for the kitchen.' That's how it is for doctors. I really did compare it to a shopping list."

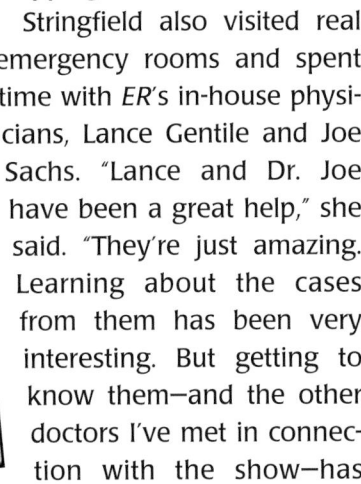

Stringfield also visited real emergency rooms and spent time with *ER*'s in-house physicians, Lance Gentile and Joe Sachs. "Lance and Dr. Joe have been a great help," she said. "They're just amazing. Learning about the cases from them has been very interesting. But getting to know them—and the other doctors I've met in connection with the show—has

been even more revealing in some ways. Doctors seem to have a resilience and patience and talent beyond what is normal for the rest of us. It's as if they have an extra gene, an extra special factor that explains why they're doctors. It's amazing. They do a job where they actually *help* someone—and that's important to all the doctors I've met, even the really tired ones. There seems to be something larger at stake, a need to make things better and find gratification in saving someone's life. Down inside there is a need to help people, and that's really rare."

On *ER* these altruistic qualities are intertwined with the characters' human frailties, a combination that Stringfield believes accounts for the show's audience appeal. "I think people feel attacked in their own lives," said Stringfield, "and I think they relate to certain characters. Benton is supporting his family and trying to do well on his own. Lewis tries to treat patients and they say, no, we want to see the *real* doctor. The show has that 'it's always something' kind of feel about it. In the case of *ER* these things are happening to doctors, who are like heroes, but the show still leaves people with the feeling that it's okay, I can make a difference, too. I don't know if that's why people watch it, but that's why I like it."

Noah Wyle / "John Carter"

Through John Carter's eyes, we register the strangeness and wonder of the emergency room. As a medical student, he bridges the gap between those who are doctors and the rest of us who merely *go* to the doctor, and reminds us all of what it feels like to be new at something completely bewildering.

As portrayed by actor Noah Wyle, Carter is an extremely moral and compassionate individual. He also happens to be very funny, a quality

Wyle began developing early on. "There were a couple of scenes in the pilot that led me to believe Carter was sort of a clumsy, slapsticky kind of guy," he recalled. "One was a scene where he is administering an IV for the first time to a policeman who has shot himself in the leg. It was written very comically. Another scene had Carter sewing up a woman's hand and he had no idea when she's supposed to come and have the stitches taken out. The nucleus for the character was in Michael Crichton's script, and I just went with it from there. I have to be careful, though. I have a tendency to sometimes make Carter clumsier and more cartoonish than he really is, just because I have fun doing it. As he matures, I'm trying to segue that same boyish, youthful naiveté away from his professional life and into his personal life. As he gets more and more comfortable in his surroundings at the hospital, he'll experience that naiveté in his personal dealings."

In preparing for his role, Wyle made the assumption that Carter was based on Crichton during his years as a medical student—a supposition the author firmly denied. "I started out by reading as many of Michael's books as possible beforehand," said Wyle, "especially *Travels*, which is an autobiographical work. When I asked him about Carter, Michael said that *all* the characters in *ER* are him, in one way or another. So then I did extensive reading in other areas. I read some wonderful books by third-year medical students who kept journals through their rotations in the emergency room. I also read various medical textbooks and a couple of straight fiction books like *House of*

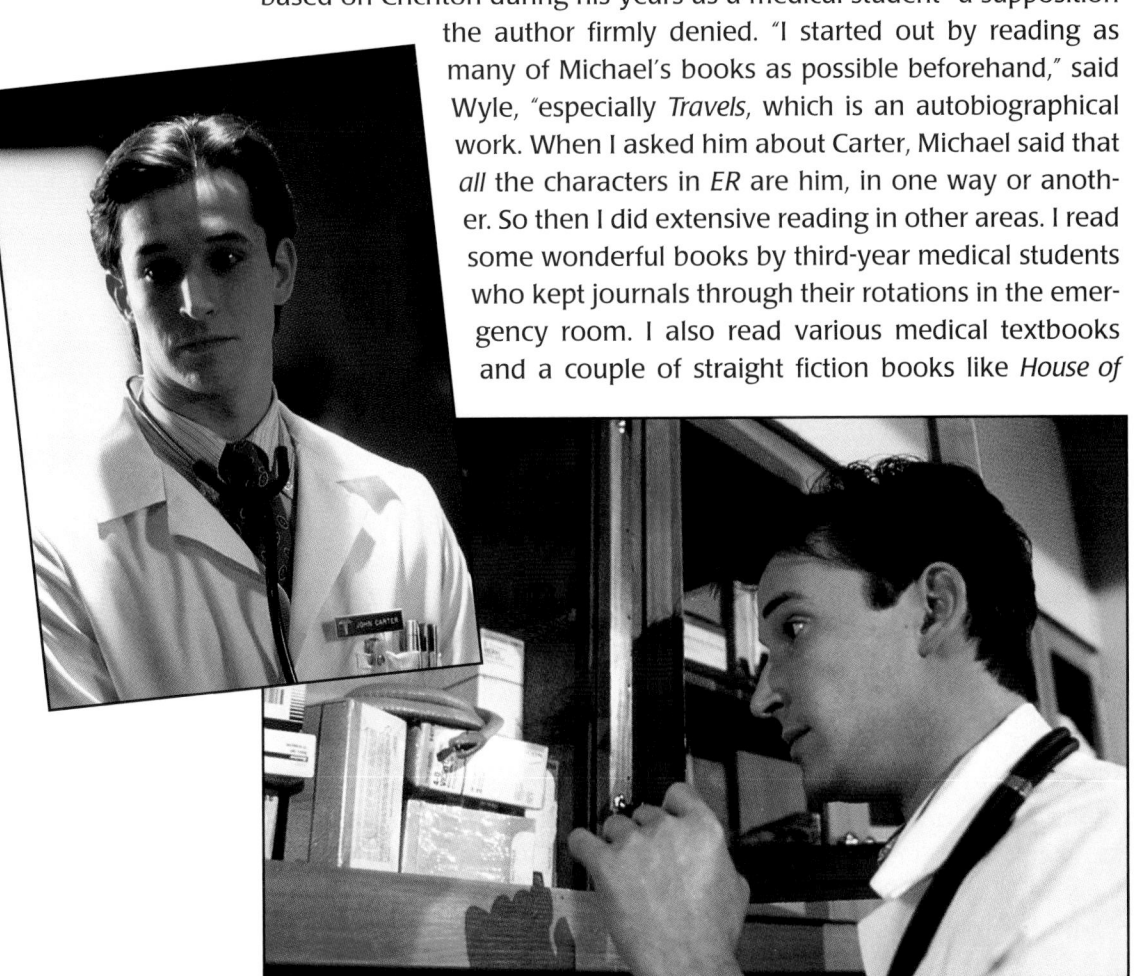

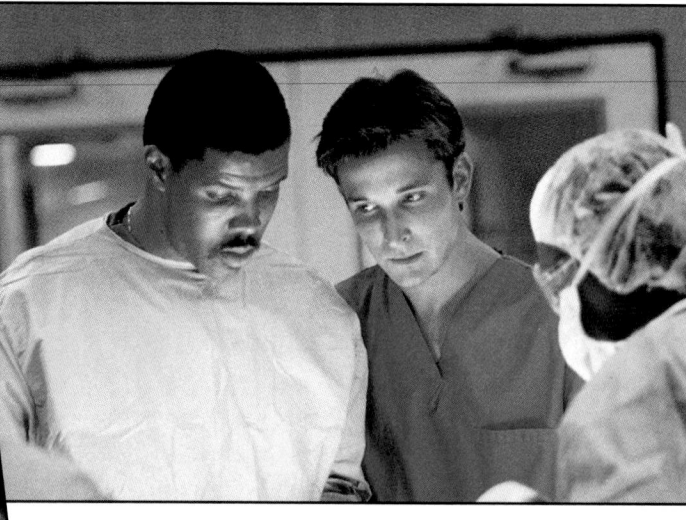

God, just to familiarize myself with the medical slang and lingo. My mother's a nurse, and I went to her hospital and hung out in the emergency room. I also spent some time running around with Lance and Joe. The research was really fun for me. It's where I picked up most of my good stuff."

As far as Wyle is concerned, the show's success results from a combination of appealing characters and the tried-and-true hospital genre. "Of course," he admitted, "we step it up a notch in terms of pace, which is something that people nowadays seem to favor. But our stories are very human, and everybody can identify with at least one of our characters per show. You've got single working mothers; you've got professional families that have no time for each other; you've got women trying to make their way in a male-dominated work environment; you've got a black man in a white bureaucratic hospital; you've got a pediatrician who, because of the pressures of seeing kids beaten every day, has a little drinking problem; and you've got a guy like Carter who, I think, everybody can identify with. We can all look back in our lives and find a time when we were thrown into a work environment we weren't adequately prepared for and constantly had to play catch-up. Everybody can relate to that."

Julianna Margulies / "Carol Hathaway"

Julianna Margulies was never meant to make it past the pilot. Her character, Carol Hathaway, takes a drug overdose during the first two hours of the show and the prognosis doesn't look good. But when it became certain that *ER* was going to be picked up by NBC, the show's producers took a good look at the positive audience response to the Hathaway character. They also considered their own feelings about losing a sensitive and talented performer and realized that Margulies was definitely *not* someone they could do without. Hathaway was discreetly resurrected and returned to work by the second episode.

Because she was intended to appear only in the pilot, however, the character was initially not as fully rounded as some of the others. For Margulies, that only made things more interesting. "As an actor," said Margulies, "I've had quite a bit of say in who Carol Hathaway is. In the pilot, we mostly saw her passing through the hallways, and wondered if she may have had a thing with Dr. Ross—and then suddenly she comes through the doors on a gurney. I was able to fill in the blanks and create a life for her outside of the writing and outside of the emergency room."

To do that, Margulies began to understand Hathaway as a complex and multilayered individual. One of her first concerns was figuring out *why* the character tried to commit suicide. "Hathaway's suicide attempt wasn't really touched on much by the producers because they felt that an emergency room was already a dark enough place and that it was important to move on. That was understandable, but it made things difficult to play truthfully. I needed to be able to get between the lines and understand the issues she was struggling with—and I wanted it to be more than her previous involvement with Ross. So everything that has gone into the character has had to do with building up her self-confidence. Actually, it's been very helpful for me, as a human being, to see Hathaway become more and more free of the demons that were in her closet."

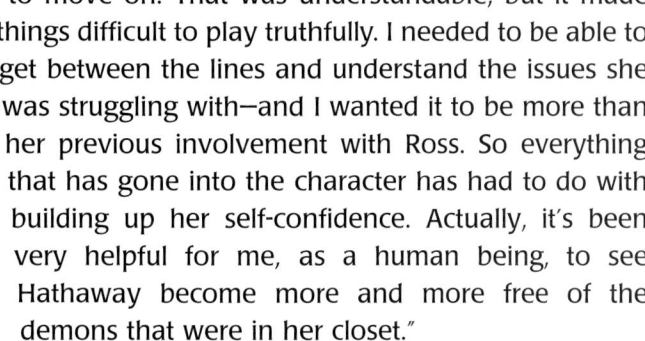

The process of understanding Carol Hathaway included research into the lives of real emergency room nurses. Beyond gaining technical and professional knowledge, Margulies developed some personal insights as well. "Nurses, especially charge nurses in the emergency room, are very much in control of their jobs," she said. "They have to be—but very often their personal lives suffer. Hathaway is no different. She is confident in her job, yet her personal life is in shambles. It seemed

apropos for Hathaway to be searching for control
or happiness in a man, because oftentimes that's what females do. 'If I
can just find Prince Charming, I'll be okay. If I can just find stability, I'll be
okay.' I think Hathaway is learning that she's not going to find happiness
in anyone except herself. She is actually a very strong individual; she just
needs to find where to go to get that strength. She's like an onion. You
just keep peeling off layers and finding new things."

Hathaway's layers have been revealed to include a sardonic sense of
humor and a powerfully felt individualism. "Hathaway is confident in
some ways," noted Margulies, "but she also has a weak side. I think she's
trying to find a balance. Along with Sherry Stringfield's character, Susan

Lewis, Hathaway has to hold her own in a predominantly male world. They are both 'no frills' kinds of women. Hathaway and Lewis have to be very male in a lot of ways, but when they are together, they get to be feminine and enjoy each other's company."

It is also significant to Margulies that Hathaway and Lewis are well-formed characters completely independent of the men on the show. "On *ER* I get to play a fully rounded woman who has no dependencies on a man. I'm not the girlfriend of, the prostitute of, the mistress of, the wife of, the sister of. I am who I am. And I feel very fortunate to play a strong woman on television. You don't see many of them in film, and I think television is really a gateway for women to be able to shine a little bit more than we're allowed to on the big screen. Interestingly, I was told I would never do television because I looked too different. No one could categorize me. I think for someone who was told that, I landed a pretty amazing gig." Amazing indeed: Margulies went on to win an Emmy.

Eriq La Salle / "Dr. Peter Benton"

Dr. Peter Benton is a little hard to like at times. He is unsmiling and unfriendly, driven, arrogant, and abrasive. He seems unduly harsh with his medical student, John Carter, and shows a decided lack of humility. He can be, in a word, irritating. Then, when we see him quietly caring for his invalid mother or holding the hand of a dying AIDS patient, it becomes impossible to hold a grudge. At times like this, Benton breaks our hearts.

Actor Eriq La Salle isn't surprised that his character is considered an enigma. "Benton is one of those characters we don't quite understand," he observed. "We wonder what makes him tick. And as you start figuring certain things out about him, you discover contradictions. In some ways that is the key to the character. As you start hating him, he'll do some-  thing that makes you love him, and as you start loving him, he'll do something to make you hate him. I think some people can see beyond the tough veneer, but in general, Benton is very no-nonsense. He is serious, dri- ven, dedicated, and very committed to what he's doing and to what he's trying to accomplish."

The show's built-in pacing—with events happening quickly in the ER while the characters' lives take place in real time—makes perfect sense to La Salle. "You can approach the story from different angles because that's the way we go through it in real life. We don't experi- ence something personal or emotional and have it over in one day. There is the rising action, the climax, and then whatever happens afterward. That mirrors life, and it gives us a nice luxury. We don't feel like we have to put everything in one episode. It gives us an opportunity to explore things."

Although La Salle had played a doctor on an earlier medical drama called *The Human Factor*, he found this previous experience irrelevant when approaching the role of Peter Benton. La Salle felt it was more important to discover the character as a person, rather than basing him on his profession. "I didn't approach Benton as a doctor; it was more a matter of finding the man. I think it had to do with my training as an actor. I knew that once you start trying to play a *doctor*, that's all you end up with. I couldn't do that. The most interesting thing was figuring out who the person is—and the bottom line is that's what people tune in to see. They tune in to see how a doctor keeps his marriage alive and does whatever he needs to do on a human level while making the life-threatening decisions of his profession. I've always found that much more intriguing. And I think that's what people connect to. Otherwise what we would have is a documentary."

While the execution of the medical dialogue was somewhat challenging in the beginning, the character's authority as a doctor came easily to La Salle. "If you study it long enough, you can say a paragraph filled with medical jargon," he said. "But I knew this ability was something that would be second nature to my character. If you're supposed to be the elite, if you're supposed to be the crème de la crème, then certain things become part of your character. For example, if I'm having a

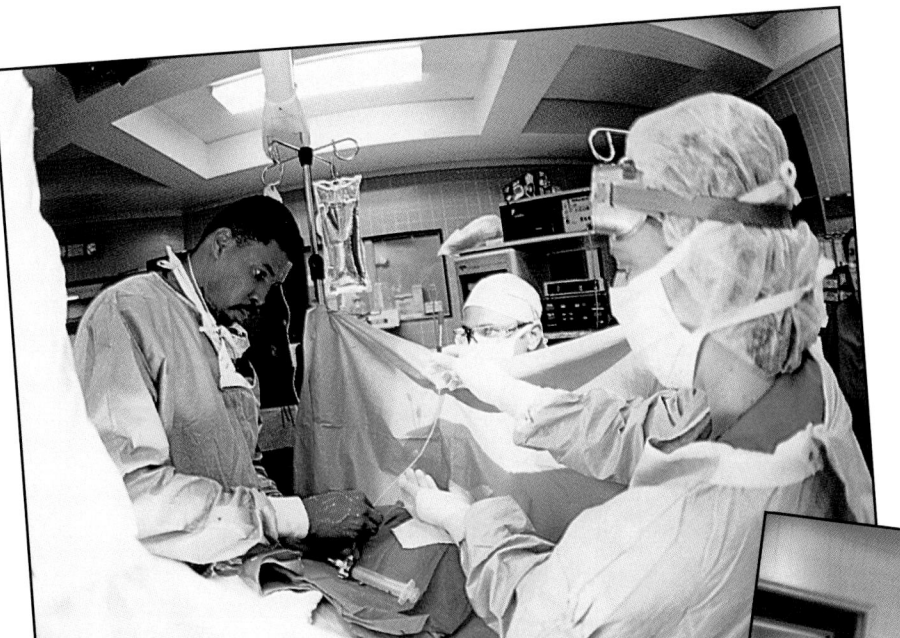

discussion about acting, I don't have to stop and think about certain words or phrases because they're part of my training—and they've been part of my training for the last fifteen years. It's the same way in the medical profession. Not only do doctors use a specific language, but there is a rapidity and flow to it. As for the command and the leadership of the doctor, that was easy; it came from the kind of man Benton is. It is possible to be a very timid doctor. But my doctor happens to be a man who is very commanding, very imposing, very straightforward, very brusque, very curt. Besides that, you're not going to ask for a thoracotomy tray as though you were asking for a Twinkie—there would be a lot more intensity to the request. By the time you get to that point, things would be a little serious."

After more than a year as Dr. Benton, La Salle can guess at a few of the reasons for *ER*'s appeal—but the truth is, he doesn't really want to know. "Obviously there are certain things that contribute to the show's success: I think we approach it from a very truthful and gritty point of view, and all that. But to me, as an artist, I like the reason to be something more intangible. I don't want it to be a recipe; I don't think art ever is. It doesn't hurt for us to be aware of our strengths—in a recipe we know sugar is sweet, we know lemons are sour—but to go on and say, 'Three tablespoons of sugar and three tablespoons of lemon will give us this,' scares me. I think, maybe even more than the first season, in the second season we will explore some things that people don't really quite get. And then again we may just go back and do what we know works. You can't really duplicate it; I wouldn't want to."

Gloria Reuben / "Jeanie Boulet"

Gloria Reuben first appeared during the middle of the first season (Episode 13, to be exact) when her character, Jeanie Boulet, was hired by Peter Benton to care for his mother, who had had a stroke. Boulet entered Benton's life as a married physical therapist and before long she and the doctor had slipped into a more serious relationship. The audience had only started to know her character when the season came to an end.

Reuben sees Jeanie Boulet as having qualities similar to those of her romantic interest on the show. "Jeanie is a lot like Benton," said Reuben. "She's very committed to her work and she really enjoys it. But she also has a lighter side than Dr. Benton, who has a tendency to be rather serious. She is obviously intelligent and sensitive, with a dry sense of humor, and is pretty clear in terms of her direction and what she wants in her life. In many ways, because she is so new to the series, Jeanie Boulet is still beginning to form, but once she's integrated with everybody else in the ER certain things about her character will pop. Of course, because of the intensity of her relationship with Benton, there are built-in avenues for character development and more forms of expression."

Reuben understands that even for the most clear-sighted among us life can sometimes get in the way. "Even though we may be sure about things, something else gets thrown into the picture and, all of a sudden, an area of our life is less certain. In that respect, Jeanie's personal life gets very jumbled as she becomes more and more involved with Peter. It's not necessarily just chemistry. Two people who work in the same stressful field can be drawn together for other reasons." Although Jeanie Boulet began as a physical therapist during the first season, she returned the second season as an aspiring physician's assistant, resulting in more direct involvement in the emergency room. Reuben knows that the life-and-death urgency of the ER can't help but affect the characters and their relationship.

The intricacies of the Boulet-Benton affair were somewhat challenging for Reuben during the second season's summertime Chicago shoot. She and La Salle were required to act out a scene from Episode 4—a scene in which their characters had clearly been involved for quite a while—without prior knowledge of the three preceding scripts. "It was a very strange situation," admitted Reuben, "but part of the fun in acting is creating and, just knowing that people who spend as much time together as Jeanie and Benton would have, I realized they would have developed a deep emotional bond. The scene we shot in Chicago was quite intense. Things were at the brim of exploding. But I just did my internal work and knew there would be an understanding and depth of emotion that comes from spending that kind of time with someone who isn't your married partner."

In preparing for her role on *ER* Reuben spent some time with a real-life physical therapist, researching both the profession and the person. "The most exciting part of all was observing how she was with her patients. I learned much more from observing *who* she was and how she dealt with people than just the technicalities of her job. There were certain things about her personality that I was able to integrate into Jeanie Boulet." Reuben followed the same research procedure in learning about the life of a physician's assistant. "It's always interesting to watch people and to see how they relate to others, especially in that kind of profession. How do their personal lives affect the way they do their work? I love that kind of thing. The technical aspects can always be learned in other ways."

Her role on *ER* represents the fulfillment of a pact Reuben made with herself not long after finishing a film for Paramount Pictures. "I promised myself that if I was going to do television, it was going to be the best of television. I decided that the only three shows I would do were *Law and Order, Homicide,* and *ER.* The following fall I was on *Homicide* for a few episodes—and then I ended up on *ER.* Incredibly, I was on two out of the three. To be a regular on *ER* is completely amazing and I'm really looking forward to being a part of the quality of it."

SUPPORTING CAST

Abraham Benrubi / "Jerry Markovic"

Although Abraham Benrubi's family was involved in the medical profession, he wasn't remotely interested in following tradition. As a child, he was drawn to a world of fantasy instead. "I grew up reading comic books and science fiction novels," he said. "I started acting by pretending to be Spider-Man in my bedroom."

An admitted escapist in his youth, Benrubi was a big fan of *Star Trek* and futuristic space movies. He can vividly recall his first impression of *Star Wars.* "The movie really changed my life. I told my parents, 'That's what I want to do when I grow up.' They thought I meant acting, but what I really meant was saving the universe."

Nonetheless, Benrubi did pursue an acting career. He began performing in his hometown of Indianapolis and ended up in Los Angeles with a regular part on *Parker Lewis Can't Lose*. A role on a pilot called *Polish Hill* (produced by John Wells) ultimately led Benrubi to *ER* and his character, Jerry Markovic.

Benrubi describes himself as a "rabid music fan," with an eclectic taste that includes everything from Beethoven to Bob Marley. He has a particular interest in music from other countries. "I'm really attracted to Celtic mythology and the music and arts of that culture," he said. "I don't know why. I have no Irish blood in me at all—my father is Greek."

Conni Marie Brazelton / "Conni Oligario"

Conni Marie Brazelton grew up in Waukegan, Illinois, and graduated from Southern Illinois University. Armed with a BA in theater, she moved from the Midwest to New York, then to Los Angeles as she pursued an acting career. After being hired for *ER*, Brazelton stayed with her good friend CCH Pounder (Dr. Angela Hicks) for nine months. "I thought I would do four episodes after the pilot," Brazelton recalled. "I ended up being in twenty-two." Brazelton decided it was time for her own place.

Brazelton's career isn't the only reason she's been pulled between L.A. and New York. Her husband, writer Michael George, is a die-hard New Yorker and maintains a residence there. "Our bicoastal relationship amazes a lot of people," said Brazelton. "But you do what you have to do. We love each other and when we're together, it's like a honeymoon all over again. We're used to it. Even our dating was bicoastal."

Besides acting, traveling, and preparing for a new baby (her real-life pregnancy was written into the script), Brazelton creates jewelry for Banji Face Jewelry, a company she owns with Pounder. "I took the name from a screenplay my husband had written called *Banji Girls*," Brazelton explained. "I found out later that *banji* means 'to walk with God.' It just fell into place." Brazelton and Pounder can frequently be seen wearing Banji Face designs on *ER*.

Ellen Crawford / "Lydia Wright"

Ellen Crawford spent most of her childhood in Normal, Illinois, where she was introduced to acting through children's theater programs at Illinois State University. "It was the best of all possible worlds," said

Crawford. "All the cultural and educational advantages of a university town in the middle of a cornfield."

Although she won the first theater scholarship to Illinois State, Crawford chose to audition for the original Chicago company of *Hair* instead. "I wanted to see what it would be like to go to a cattle call," she said. "There were thirty-five hundred people auditioning. I went up there looking pretty straight, but the lake air frizzed my hair." Crawford was hired for the show. Several years later, she went back to school and graduated from Carnegie Mellon.

Crawford has played a variety of extreme characters, from a werewolf to a Southern baby merchant to the murderous Clytemnestra. On *ER*, she finds it a pleasure to play someone so close to home. "It's easy to step into Lydia Wright's skin," Crawford noted. "Like her, I come from a midwestern, no-nonsense kind of community. I've never wanted to be a nurse, but I have tremendous admiration for what they do. Actors are perpetual students, and it's been wonderful to learn so much about that walk of life."

Crawford is married to Michael Genovese, a veteran actor who has a recurring role on *ER* as Sergeant Al Grabarsky. Together they enjoy camping, bicycling, and spending time with their family.

Deezer D. / "Malik McGrath"

Deezer D.'s dream was to become a professional basketball player, but when he got kicked off his high school team, things changed. He dropped out of school and began hanging out with a bad crowd. Soon after, he developed a problem with alcohol.

A friend introduced Deezer to the idea of working as an extra. As he provided background atmosphere for commercials, television, and films, Deezer was determined to become an actor. He pursued his interest in music and, hoping for a record deal, wrote and recorded rap. An antismoking rap led to a commercial, which led to an agent—and the chance he had been hoping for.

After his career got going, Deezer appeared in *China Beach* and *Angel Street*, both produced by John Wells. "I told John I'd like to work with him again," Deezer recalled, "and he said okay. At the time, I didn't know he was a huge producer. I just thought he was some cool guy."

Deezer began attending Alcoholics Anonymous meetings and stopped drinking. He was working on a drug-and-alcohol counselor internship when his agent called. "He said, 'You remember John Wells?

He wants you to play Malik on *ER*.' John kept his promise."

Deezer recently completed a new rap album, something people from his old neighborhood said he would never do. "I lived a rough life," he said. "It's very easy to get caught up in the ways of the inner city. But there's so much to see in this world, and so much to do. I got a break and I took advantage of it."

Yvette Freeman / "Haleh Adams"

Yvette Freeman was raised in a house of music. Her father was a piano player and his legacy was a love of jazz. "I would sing with my father whenever I could," Freeman recalled, "but he said, 'You have to go to college.' So I did."

Freeman earned a bachelor's degree in art (she recently completed illustrating a children's book) and then embarked on her career as a performer. She appeared in *Ain't Misbehavin'* on Broadway and later toured with the show—and many others. "I did every musical on the road that there is," she said. Freeman has had singing engagements in Paris, Monte Carlo, and the States. During *ER*'s summer hiatus, she appeared in *Dinah Was*, a play with music based on the life of jazz singer Dinah Washington.

After years on the road, Freeman settled down in Los Angeles and began appearing on television shows, frequently playing nurses. She gained insight into nursing while caring for her father before his death. "Taking care of my father taught me about giving love and opening my heart—and being dedicated."

Freeman's theatrical experience proved useful in a different way. "Being a stage actress helps me with all the choreography and timing on *ER*," she said. "It also prepared me for working in an ensemble. I can be just as happy in the background knowing that I'm helping somebody else shine. I know my job is just as important."

Lily Mariye / "Lily Jarvik"

Lily Mariye's ability to sing, dance, and act brought her to Los Angeles when she was seventeen. She earned a BA in theater from UCLA while auditioning for jobs on stage. In 1982, her performance in an Equity-waiver musical caught the attention of an agent who said, "I hate this show, but who's that little Chinese girl?" The next thing she knew, Mariye was in a movie: *The Best Little Whorehouse in Texas*.

While she has done plenty of television and film since then, *ER* represents Mariye's first continuing role in a series. "The show's success is amazing," she noted, "but all I see is the day-to-day work. We aren't focused on, 'What can we do to make people watch us?' We're focused on, 'How can we do the best job possible?' "

Mariye has two older brothers, one of whom has cerebral palsy. "Eugene has been in a wheelchair most of his life," she said. "And it's given me a real empathy for people who have to deal with hospitals and illness." Moreover, her father died of a heart attack when she was seven and her mother suffered from Alzheimer's disease. "It's very personal for me to portray someone in the medical field. These people have courage and compassion—while at the same time, spines of steel. It's a lot like acting. You have to have an artistic, vulnerable side and yet be able to deal with the rigors of the business."

Mariye has been married for ten years to Boney James, a jazz musician who just released his third album.

Vanessa Marquez / "Wendy Goldman"

Perseverance paid off for Vanessa Marquez.

She knew she wanted to act when she was four years old and by the time she was eight, had begun to write letters to casting directors, producers, and agents. In her early teens she started working as an extra. By age eighteen, she had sent out so many pictures and résumés that somebody finally paid attention. She was hired for *Stand and Deliver* and has been acting professionally ever since.

Marquez is a part-time college student, working toward a degree in theater history and literature at Cal State Los Angeles. She also studies voice and is particularly fond of musical theater and blues. Surprisingly, she has taken only a couple of acting classes. "By the time I was in college," Marquez explained, "I had done a lot of theater and worked with some really incredible actors. Acting classes made me feel self-conscious. As part of a cast, I was treated as a peer and not as a student. I really learned by doing."

Learning by doing is part of Marquez's personal philosophy as well. She became a volunteer for the United Farm Workers in 1988, marching and picketing alongside Cesar Chavez. She has spoken for Amnesty International and campaigned for several presidential candidates. "I like to do political-social work," said Marquez. "If it fires me up, I'll get involved."

ER's Eight Emmy Awards
TIES RECORD FOR MOST BY A FRESHMAN SERIES

ER, Warner Bros. Television's freshman drama series, won eight Emmy Awards, tying the record set by *Hill Street Blues* in 1981 for most by a first-year series.

CONSTANT c / AMBLIN TELEVISION / WARNER BROS. TELEVISION

Outstanding supporting actress in a drama series
Julianna Margulies

Outstanding individual achievement in writing in a drama series
Lance Gentile

Outstanding individual achievement in directing in a drama series
Mimi Leder,
DIRECTOR—*LOVE'S LABOR LOST*

Outstanding individual achievement in casting
Barbara Miller, CSA,
EXECUTIVE IN CHARGE OF CASTING
John Levey, CSA,
VICE PRESIDENT, TALENT CASTING

Outstanding individual achievement in editing for a series—single camera production
Randy Jon Morgan and Rick Tuber

Outstanding individual achievement in graphic design and title sequences
Billy Pittard, SENIOR TITLE DESIGNER
Suzanne Kiley, PRINCIPAL TITLE DESIGNER

Outstanding individual achievement in sound mixing for a drama series
Russell Fager, PRODUCTION SOUND MIXER
Michael E. Jiron, SOUND EFFECTS MIXER
Allen L. Stone, DIALOGUE MIXER
Frank Jones, MUSIC MIXER

Outstanding individual achievement in sound editing for a series
Walter Newman,
SUPERVISING SOUND EDITOR
John Bonds, Rick Camera, Steve Sax,
SOUND EFFECTS EDITORS
John Reynolds, Catherine Flynn,
DIALOGUE EDITORS
Tom Harris, ADR EDITOR, Susan Mick,
MUSIC EDITOR

Chapter 6
Postproduction

For some members of the *ER* production team, the final day of filming an episode is only the beginning. As the actors, producers, and director are turning their attention to a brand-new script, the film, sound, and music editing departments have just begun to shape the unfinished visual images into a complete and cohesive form.

Because of the cyclical nature of television production, postproduction technically begins during the eight-day shoot as the show's footage is examined on a day-to-day basis. Film that is shot on a Monday, for example, is developed and transferred onto tape during the night, and is ready to view by lunchtime on Tuesday. To gain a better understanding of what has been captured on film—and to keep abreast of changes, modifications, or potential problems—the producers, director, and film editor gather every afternoon in John Wells's office for the cinematic ritual more familiarly known as watching dailies. Also present are Lance Gentile, who monitors the film for medical accuracy, and associate producer Wendy Spence, who is responsible for overseeing *ER*'s exhaustive postproduction phase.

To keep up with the fast-paced schedule, Randy Jon Morgan alternates film editing duties with Jacque Toberen, who joined the show during the second season. Jim Gross shared the editing job with Morgan during the first season, but left *ER* to join another well-received series, *The X-Files*. Editing assignments are divided into odd- and even-numbered shows to accommodate the overlap between postproduction on one show and production on another. Essentially, every sixteenth day an editor is ready to start looking at dailies for a new episode.

Editor Randy John Morgan—who received an Emmy for his outstanding work on ER—and Mimi Leder at work in the editing room.

The editors begin linking together rough images of the story on a daily basis during the eight-day shoot, so that by the ninth day—the day after the final day of filming on any given episode—they have a "first assembly" ready to show the director. "Sometimes we might need an extra day or so, given the nature of a particular show," said Morgan, who was also responsible for editing the pilot. "We then spend anywhere from two to four days with the director. The rest of the time we confer with John Wells and the producers—as well as with the studio, the network, Michael Crichton, and Steven Spielberg—who look at the show and give us their comments and suggestions."

The editors find themselves representing two diametrically opposed forces as they approach each episode: one as storytellers and the other as the show's first audience. "I rarely read the script beforehand," Morgan said. "So when I look at the dailies I try to find the best way of trying to tell the story as written, given the film that's been shot. The editor is very much a storyteller. He just tells the story with pieces of film rather than with words. On the other hand, as the first audience, I'm always waiting to see what's going to happen next. I rarely go into a scene with any preconceived notions as to the form it will take." Morgan follows the lead suggested by the material rather than trying to impose a different structural style. "I like to go with the flow. Sometimes it works to go against the grain just a little bit.

Award-winning ADR editor Tom Harris and associate producer Wendy Spence working on the ADR stage.

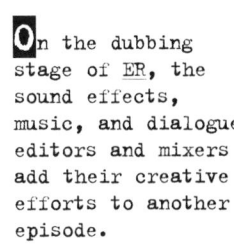

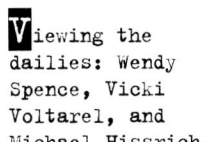
Viewing the dailies: Wendy Spence, Vicki Voltarel, and Michael Hissrich.

That can add some tension or excitement where maybe a scene is lacking in pace, but by and large it's the way the material is handled by the director that dictates how the editor is going to edit the scene."

Editor Rick Tuber, also an Emmy recipient, assists during the postproduction process. Tuber is responsible for editing the trailers that tell the audience what is coming "Next on *ER*," as well as the recaps that tell what has happened previously on the show. During the first season, Tuber and Morgan coedited "Love's Labor Lost" and the visually complex "Blizzard" episode, both directed by Mimi Leder.

On the dubbing stage of ER, the sound effects, music, and dialogue editors and mixers add their creative efforts to another episode.

The film editors use the Avid Editing System which, technically speaking, doesn't process lengths of film at all, but computerized electronic images. During the "telecine" process, when the dailies are transferred from film to tape, a three-quarter-inch tape is made for the editing department so they can digitize the footage and input it into the Avid. The computer incorporates all the film and sound on a digital level, which then provides an instant recall process. This allows the editors to assemble the footage in any way they choose and to work more quickly and efficiently than they could using the old-fashioned method of literally splicing together assorted lengths of film.

The Avid proved to be particularly useful in the "Blizzard" episode when a complicated montage was called for. The episode depicts the emergency room staff creatively coping with the woes of boredom and then suddenly having to prepare to treat dozens of incoming injured upon receiving the news of a major traffic disaster. Leder shot considerable footage of the characters going through the motions of setting up triage and obtaining supplies. The question was how best to assemble the film to achieve the optimum visual and emotional impact.

Initially, Morgan put together a straightforward montage (a rapid sequence of images) of the footage. "It just seemed like there could be something more that we could bring to the scene," he said. "So I started dissolving the shots together, which seemed to give a whole new feel to the material. Then Mimi shot some additional pans of the hospital showing the same action, but on a wider scope. After we had designed a dissolve montage of the principal action, we then laid these long pans over that action, and it gave a multilayered impressionistic kind of vision—which was much more intense than it would have been had we simply cut the shots together. Using traditional editing techniques, we would have more likely gone with a simple cutting montage. The Avid allowed us to construct something much more intricate and, hopefully, give the audience a more intense viewing experience."

The edited footage contains only the dialogue track obtained during filming. No heart monitors, breathing noises, background clatter, or musical elements are present during this phase. While cutting the picture, the editor will usually include whatever temporary sound effects and music seem necessary to present the show in the best possible way, but nothing else is added. "My philosophy is to cut it as naked as I possibly can," said Morgan, "with only principal dialogue and whatever minimal effects—for example, an elevator sound effect—are necessary to help clarify what's going on. I basically like to run the show for the director and the producers without any sound at all, except for what's absolutely essential, so that they're not swayed unduly by all the fancy footwork. If they buy it that way, then the sound effects and music are only going to make it better."

Once the show is locked into its forty-five-minute running length, the postproduction department kicks into high gear under the supervision of Wendy Spence. The film is cut and color-corrected. The sound effects and music—along with additional dialogue and background tracks—are then laid into each episode and adjusted to the appropriate levels during the final sound mix.

To begin with, Spence distributes spotting cassettes of the visually completed episode to the various postproduction film and sound departments. Each spotting cassette is equipped with time-coded specifications striped onto the videotape for accurate reference by the individual departments. She then has a music spotting session with composer Marty Davich, music editor Susan Mick, the writer for the episode, John Wells, Mimi Leder, and Christopher Chulack. Ideas are discussed and suggestions made as to the best way to cue the music to the visual images. Davich then returns to his studio and composes the entire episode, usually within three days. "The music needs to be a part of the picture," Spence noted. "If you're thinking about the music, then you've lost touch with the story. If you feel the music—and you really understand what it's trying to say—it blends in with everything else. Marty does a seamless job. Each week he performs something different, something new with a little edge to it."

The producers make certain the music is used judiciously to flavor the show without becoming routine. "We don't want the show to sound too 'cue-y' by using obvious music cues for specific situations," Spence continued. "For example, we don't want to put in a piano cue every time someone gets sad. We're very choosy about where we *place* the music—as well as how it sounds." Davich lays the music cues onto a rough version of the videotape followed by more input from the producers. The final approved music cues are then prelayed by Susan Mick onto the show's master track and later mixed into the final sound track.

While Davich is busy composing, Spence conducts a sound effects spotting session with sound supervisor Walter Newman, the sound editors, Mimi Leder, the episode writer, and Lance Gentile. Together, they go through the tape discussing the aesthetics of each scene and determining the audio cues that will enrich the picture with another layer of realism. For example, the background sound of an El train might be added to a shot, or footsteps, medical clatter, and harried voices to a trauma scene. Gentile is on hand to make sure that sounds of respirators and heart monitors are appropriately and accurately placed.

"When we get the final cut, the only sound recorded on the production track is the dialogue," said Spence. "We creatively and very intentionally add everything else in postproduction. The dialogue is very important, of course, and we always work to protect the words because they tell the story along with the visual picture, but the extraneous sounds really color the experience and make you feel like you're a part of the doctors' world."

Walter Newman designs an exceptional sound track in a remarkably short amount of time, coordinating with an award-winning team of sound effects editors John Bonds, Rick Camera, and Steve Sax; dialogue editors Catherine Flynn and Tom Harris; and foley artist Casey Crabtree. Newman draws from a library of sound effects that are loaded into a digitally based computer that breaks the elements down by sound bytes and time codes. The effects are then multilayered onto separate tracks and very specifically placed to coordinate with the action on screen by the effects editors. The foley, which includes all the footsteps and any other movement made by the characters, is recorded on another track.

The editors then create a cue sheet that matches the effects to specific codes, and assists effects mixer Michael Jiron in easily keeping track of cues during the final mixing stage. Further layers are added to the master track by Flynn, who makes sure the words for every episode are clear and understandable, and by Harris, who manages the ADR, or Automated Dialogue Replacement.

In precomputer times, a process called "looping" was used to add dialogue to the film during postproduction. An actor would listen to a scene played over and over again on a continuous loop, and then record his lines in sync with the film. This was used to correct garbled or unclear dialogue and to embellish scenes as necessary for clarification. ADR follows the same basic process as looping, but employs a computer to determine the exact frame where a line begins and the exact frame where it ends. Though technically different, the ADR process is still frequently referred to as looping.

One entire day is spent looping each episode of *ER*. A five-person—two female, three male—loop group called "Insync" works with Spence and Harris to add the layers of general background conversation called "walla"—

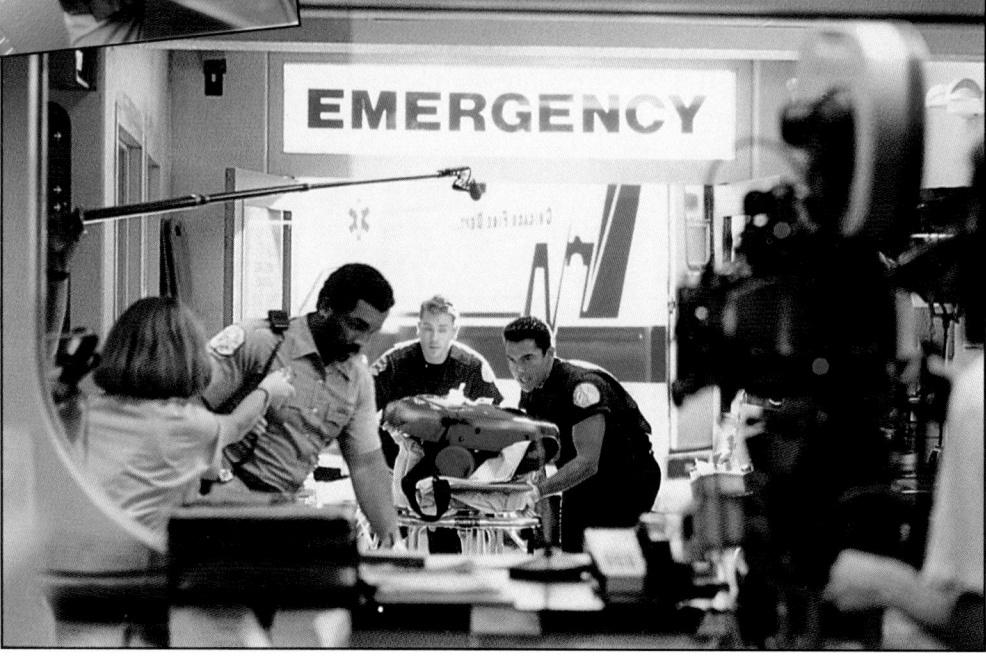

During postproduction, all sound except dialogue is added, including the noise of a trauma scene, objects breaking, the beep of medical equipment, and harried background conversation.

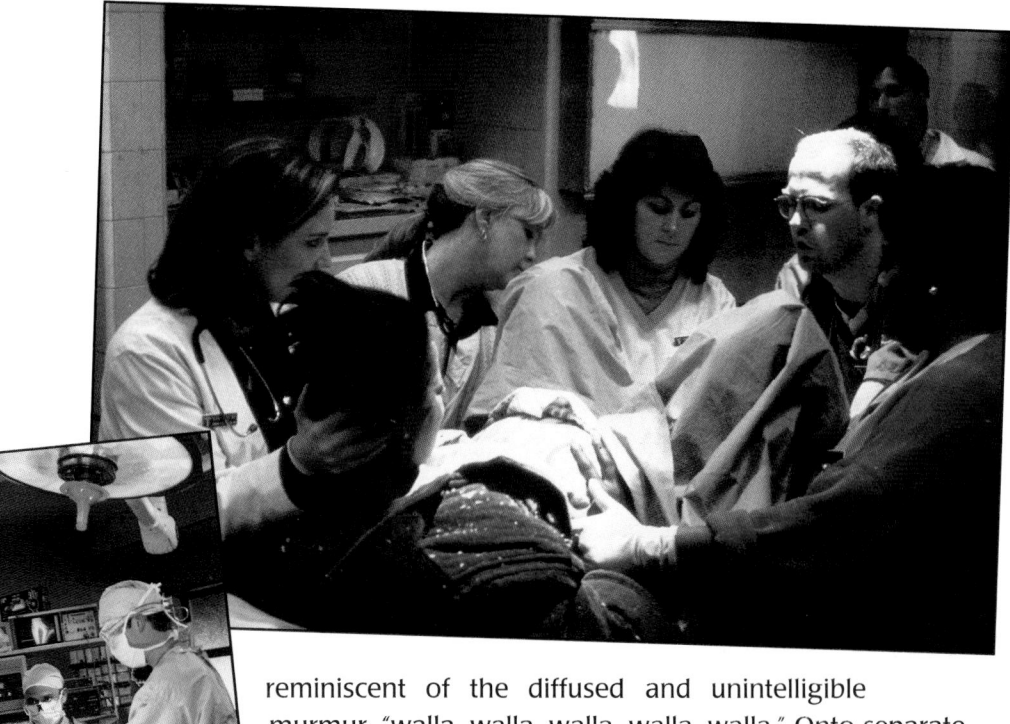

reminiscent of the diffused and unintelligible murmur, "walla, walla, walla, walla, walla." Onto separate tracks are added "general spikes," or specific lines of dialogue that can be easily understood above the walla. Lance Gentile observes the tapes and writes the additional medical dialogue according to the needs of the scene. If the scene indicates a patient going into cardiac arrest, for instance, Gentile will make specific reference to it in the dialogue and have a nurse's voice call out, "Get the crash cart!" as a general spike. Moans, groans, sneezes, and sighs are also contributed as necessary.

Occasionally the principal actors are required to do ADR as well. "John Wells or the writer may decide that we need an additional line of dialogue for clarification," said Spence, "and the actors will have to come back and do ADR. Our production mixer tries to record the dialogue as 'clean' as possible, but sometimes there's a technical problem that happens on stage during filming—say, a clipboard clamps down when someone is saying their line or maybe they weren't adequately miked. The hardest thing is to get the actors off the stage because their time is so limited. The daily shooting schedule is such that we may get the actors on their only break in the day. Even so, our cast is most accommodating—and they're all great loopers."

The producers and editors don't necessarily use all the ADR recorded. "Once we're in the final mixing stage," continued Spence, "the original production may sound more true to life with the flaws imbedded

in the track. If we extract the flaws and add the newly recorded dialogue, it can often sound intrusive. Lots of times we live with what we've got."

Reality is further enhanced during postproduction by the almost subliminal layers of "Chicago-ese" that are added to the master tape. The sound of a local traffic report or popular Chicago DJs may be heard on the radio at the admit desk. The loop group will make references to real Chicago events in the walla or add general spikes. These thoughtful elements add to the realistic texture of the show.

"We don't like to ADR scenes if we don't have to," said Spence, "because we can lose the nuances of an actor's original performance. Unfortunately, we sometimes have no choice. For example, we may have a scene where a helicopter lands and drops off a critically injured patient and the dialogue will be completely unintelligible because of the volume of the helicopter during the shoot. In cases like that, we must take the entire original sound track away and start over with the naked picture. We will cue each and every line in the scene and the actors will rerecord the written dialogue to the picture on the ADR stage." The sound effects editors then have to re-create the sound of the incoming helicopter, all exterior ambiance such as snow, wind, or rain, and the sounds of sirens, gurneys, helicopter doors, and so on. In the final mix, all of these sounds and background noises are cleverly balanced to create room for the dialogue to be heard.

While Spence and the various audio departments work out the layers of sound for each episode, postproduction supervisor Michael Hissrich oversees the elements that go into finalizing the film itself: negative cutting, transferring the film to tape, color timing, doing 'dirt fixes' to eliminate any imperfections or scratches, and titling. As soon as an episode locks, a team of five negative cutters, under the direct supervision of Jeri Bennett, begin the process of cutting the original film negative and splicing it together in the proper order. They use both the final Avid cut EDL (edit decision list) and a spotting tape as a reference to carefully match each frame, making certain that every negative is cut to the exact specifications determined by the editor.

After the negative is cut, Hissrich and telecine operator Fred Eldridge spend an intensive twelve-hour day transferring the film to tape. At the same time, they correct the color using a computerized process to balance footage that was shot at different times and on different days but must appear to have taken place throughout the course of a single day, or even a few hours. Balancing the color makes the picture much richer. "A lot of shows 'on line' the dailies to a master tape and then color-correct the picture in a tape-to-tape duplicating process," said Spence. "We don't. We transfer our original negative to tape, and in doing that have a lot more range, see more depth, and create a much richer picture. You can really see what our director of photography captured on film." After the color correction, Hissrich runs a four- to six-hour session doing the dirt fixes. This master tape is then titled, with all the credits laid onto the opening and closing of the show.

Once all sound elements are completed, they are mixed together during the

Sound mixer Will Yarborough at work.

phase known as "dubbing," a term that commonly refers to the practice of duplicating tape. In this case, however, dubbing is the process of mixing together the separate elements of dialogue, sound effects, and music into one complete package.

Spence heads the dubbing sessions, where dialogue mixer Allen Stone, music mixer Frank Jones, and effects mixer Michael Jiron combine the separate audio elements. Working individual sound boards, the three mixers adjust multiple dimmerlike switches that fade the sound levels up and down in precise coordination with the picture. They refer to cue sheets that plot out exactly where the various sounds belong, laying down track after track onto the A master, which contains all the separate sounds mixed together on one tape. After two exhaustive days, most typically the Monday and Tuesday of the week the show is to be aired, they have finished the complicated task and have a playback session where the episode is viewed in its entirety.

For one last time, John Wells, Wendy Spence, the writer and director for the show, and as many producers as are available watch the episode prior to airing. Lance Gentile is also present to make sure every medical element is as correct as it can possibly be. "If a monitor goes off and it's the wrong monitor," said Gentile, "I can let them know in time to make a correction. Sometimes a breathing machine doesn't sound right. Or we might hear a respirator when there is clearly no respirator present. Occasionally, sounds may be heightened for dramatic impact, which is fine—they just can't be the wrong sounds. It's my job to make sure that the line between realistic and dramatic license stays fairly true with respect to the medicine." Final adjustments, if any, are made very carefully at this point. Any lowering in volume of a heart monitor, for example, will cause the music to sound too loud. Unraveling a trauma scene can take hours.

The final layback—where the completed picture is married to the completed sound track—immediately follows. By Wednesday at noon each week's episode has been perfected by an extremely dedicated group of people and is hand-delivered by Spence to NBC in time for its Thursday air date.

The next day, the cycle begins again.

In its first season, *ER* became the highest-ranking new drama in history and was seen by thirty-five million people each week. It ranked as the highest-rated first-year series since 1988 when *Roseanne* premiered and the highest-rated new drama since *Charlie's Angels* in 1976. *ER* received awards from a variety of organizations, including the People's Choice, the American Society of Cinematographers, the Directors Guild, the National

Kidney Foundation, the Television Critics Association, and the Viewers for Quality Television. When Emmy nominations were announced for the 1994–1995 season, *ER* had garnered a phenomenal twenty-three; it went on to win eight, tying the record for most by a first-year series.

"The perception has always been that a show like this can be critically well received, but not successful," Wells noted. "Much to our surprise, *ER* has been both. During an awards ceremony, one of the network executives actually thanked me and said that because of the success of *ER*, he felt that it made room for other shows with the same kind of integrity. I hope that's true."

Despite such critical acclaim—and an audience so devoted that missed episodes are lamented with a phone call to the studio—it remains difficult to define *ER*'s formula for success. Its elements are so varied that simple conclusions are impossible.

For Steven Spielberg, much of the credit goes to the audience that tunes in every Thursday night. "The audience has been able to grasp the slightest hint of character involvement and make a meal out of it," he said. "The show is very independently produced and written, and I think the writers do some wonderfully economical writing. Some of the most moving moments have been those very quiet, tender moments when characters resolve their relationships with very few words. There are some very powerful emotions that are really between the lines, and it's because the cast and the directors and the writers really understand who these people are."

For Michael Crichton, after waiting so many years to see his screenplay produced, the success of *ER* remains something of a mystery. "Both in real life and on the show, an ER is about people caring for one another. We live in a society where the sense of human caring, the fact that we are related to one another in a web of feeling and action, is not often expressed. The doctors and nurses on *ER* aren't perfect people, but they do their best, and they care for the people they come in contact with. *ER* often has a bittersweet flavor, but it's the real world, and it's a human world. And in its own oblique way, I think the show talks about our highest aspirations for ourselves and each other."

From Student to Physician:
Stages of Medical Education and Training

A **medical student** is someone who has received a bachelor's degree and entered a four-year graduate program (medical school) leading toward a medical doctor (MD) degree. Usually, the first two years of medical school are spent in the classroom, and the final two years are spent in a clinical setting where the student can experience more hands-on learning. A medical student is not a doctor—a distinction meticulously noted within the medical community—but may be referred to as "Doctor" in front of patients. A license to practice medicine requires an additional year as an intern in a teaching hospital. John Carter was a third-year medical student the first season. He returned the second season as a fourth-year medical student doing a surgical sub-I (sub-internship), which is a more intensive training program that functions something like an audition prior to entering an internship.

An **intern** is someone who has received an MD and is continuing to study in the hospital setting during his or her first year out of medical school. An intern is licensed to practice medicine only within the hospital and can write prescriptions. It is possible to leave the hospital after a year and go into private practice, but most doctors choose to continue their education as residents.

Theoretically speaking, an intern fills the

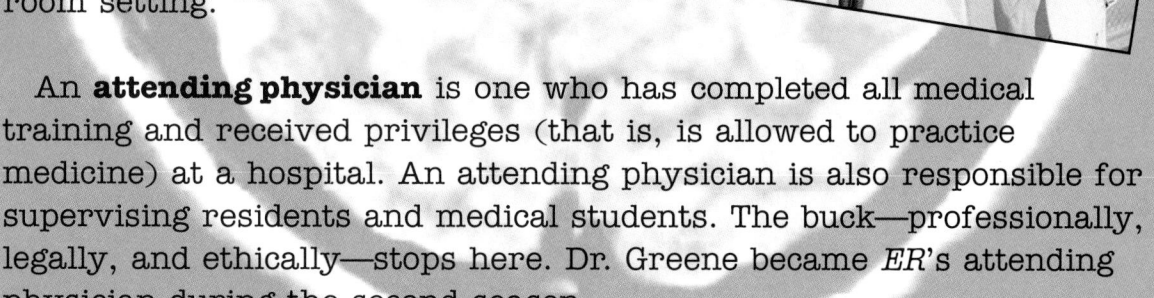

slot that might otherwise be allotted to a "first-year resident." The hospital residency program begins with the rank of second-year **resident** and involves specialized training in areas such as surgery, pediatrics, internal medicine, and psychiatry. Residencies last from two to six years, depending on the specialty. The first season, Dr. Peter Benton was a second-year surgical resident; Dr. Susan Lewis was a second-year resident in emergency medicine; and Dr. Mark Greene was a fourth-year emergency medicine resident and chief resident of the ER. Interns and residents are hospital employees, and are sometimes referred to as house officers or HOs.

A **fellowship** may or may not follow a residency. Fellowships are sought by doctors who want to specialize more completely in areas such as endocrinology, gastroenterology, or cardiology. For example, Dr. Doug Ross is a pediatric fellow in emergency medicine, which means that he spent three years in a pediatric residency, became a full-fledged pediatrician, and decided to go back for further training in emergency pediatrics in order to work strictly as a pediatrician in an emergency room setting.

An **attending physician** is one who has completed all medical training and received privileges (that is, is allowed to practice medicine) at a hospital. An attending physician is also responsible for supervising residents and medical students. The buck—professionally, legally, and ethically—stops here. Dr. Greene became *ER*'s attending physician during the second season.

ER:
Glossary of Medical Terms

ABG: Arterial blood gases. A test where blood is drawn and measured for oxygen content. The ABG tells the physician whether or not the patient is getting enough oxygen into the bloodstream. An ABG is frequently used for cases of asthma, COPD, or chest trauma.

Adenosine: A drug used to treat certain heart arrhythmias (irregular heartbeats) by helping to stabilize heart rhythm. (see **IV push**)

Angioplasty: A surgical procedure in which a small catheter with a balloon tip is threaded into the coronary artery. The balloon is then blown up to re-expand the clotted artery. (Example: "Do you want to inject **TPA** or find a cardiologist for **angioplasty**?")

Atropine: A drug used to speed up the heart rate. (Example: "Heart rate's still low. Give him another milligram of **atropine**.")

Blood culture: A test where blood is drawn and cultured for bacteria. It is usually ordered when someone has a high fever, particularly a young child, to identify the organism causing the disease and treat it with the proper antibiotic.

Blood gases: A test that determines the oxygen and carbon dioxide levels in the blood, as well as the pH. (Example: "Nothing's right with this guy. His **blood gases** stink.")

Cardiac enzymes: A damaged heart muscle releases enzymes over a period of time and, by drawing cardiac enzymes, it is possible to confirm that a heart attack has taken place. (see **coag panel**)

Cath lab: Short for catheterization laboratory, where a cardiologist performs angioplasty.

cbc: Complete blood count.

CC: Chief complaint. (Example: "**CC**'s a lingering cough and a runny nose.")

Chem 7: A blood test that measures the basic electrolytes in blood: sodium, chloride, potassium, carbon dioxide, blood urea nitrogen (BUN), creatinine, and glucose. A chem 7 is useful in the assessment of many diseases, as derangement of these elements can be fatal. (see **coag panel**)

Chest: Short for chest X ray, typically done when the doctor suspects pneumonia or to rule out pneumonia.

CHF: Congestive heart failure.

Coag panel: An assessment of how well the blood is coagulating. (Example: "Let's get a **chem 7**, **cardiac enzymes**, and **coag panel**.")

COPD: Chronic obstructive pulmonary disease.

Crit (hematocrit): A test to measure the number of red blood cells in the blood—the level of which typically decreases when a person has been bleeding or has anemia. (see **platelets**)

Diaphoresis: Sweaty skin associated with an MI. (Example: "Classic heart attack symptoms. Sudden onset, crushing substernal chest pain radiating down left arm with **diaphoresis**.")

Dopamine: A drug that makes the heart pump more strongly.

EMT: Emergency Medical Technician. (Example: "Seventy-nine-year-old male, probable heart attack. **EMT**s are two minutes away.")

Hyperresonant: When percussing (thumping) a patient's back and listening for breath sounds, the doctor will hear hyperresonant, or increased, vibrations that are indicative of a pneumothorax. (see **tension pneumo**)

Hypertension: High blood pressure.

Hypotension: Low blood pressure.

Intubation tray: A tray that contains various instruments used to intubate a patient who is not breathing: a laryngoscope, which is an instrument for opening the larynx; and an endotracheal tube, which is inserted into the trachea through the mouth to facilitate breathing. A bag is attached outside the mouth so that breathing can be done mechanically for the patient—in a procedure referred to as "bagging."

IV push: When a drug is put directly into the IV all at once. (Example: "He's relatively stable; let's try **adenosine**, six milligrams **IV push**.")

Large-bore IV: An IV with a large needle used to transfuse fluids—either saline or blood—very quickly, particularly in trauma cases, where the patient may have lost a lot of blood. (see **normal saline**)

Lavage: Washing out. A gastric lavage, for example, involves removing the bad drugs from an overdose by washing out the stomach, giving charcoal afterward, and managing the adverse side effects. A peritoneal lavage is a test for abdominal bleeding wherein blood is washed out of the abdominal cavity.

LOC: Level of consciousness. (Example: "She has an altered **LOC** from head trauma.")

MI: Myocardial infarction (heart attack). (see **ST wave**)

MVA: Motor vehicle accident.

Normal saline: Saline solution that has the same balance as the fluids in the body. Saline is administered when the patient requires fluids due to dehydration or when nothing may be taken by mouth because of the possibility of impending surgery. (Example: "He's in shock. Start two **large-bore IV**s, **normal saline**, wide open.")

Platelets: The factors in the blood that cause clotting. (Example: "Mrs. Packer's **crit** is sixteen. Her **white count**'s down to fifteen hundred, **platelets** are sixty thousand. She needs a transfusion.")

Pneumothorax: Collapsed lung.

Sinus rhythm: Normal heartbeat. (Example: "He went into **sinus rhythm** as the EMTs pulled up.")

ST wave: On a heart monitor, one heartbeat is reflected as a PQRST wave. A segment of that wave is the ST. (Example: "His **ST wave** is way up. Acute **MI**. We are in trouble.")

Tension pneumo: Short for tension pneumothorax. It is a collapsed lung where air escapes into the chest every time the patient breathes, as if through a one-way valve. A tension pneumo can cause pressure on the heart and is a serious emergency. (Example: "No breath sounds, **hyperresonant** on the left side. He's got a **tension pneumo.**")

Throat swab: A throat swab is the same as a throat culture and is used to test for Streptococcus.

Tox screen/RUDS: Blood tests to determine what drugs a person took. RUDS is short for Random Urine Drug Screen.

TPA: A powerful drug used to dissolve a blood clot in the coronary artery that is causing a heart attack. (see **angioplasty**)

V-tach: When the heart is beating at an abnormally high rate. (Example: "If this rhythm is **v-tach**, we need to shock him.")

White count: A test to measure the number of white blood cells in the blood. The white cells are the blood cells that fight infection, and an increased count usually indicates the presence of an infection. (see **platelets**)

Glossary of Slang Terms

Acute MI: Acute monetary insufficiency.

Baby doll: Vaginal bleeder.

Bag 'em: Put someone on a respirator.

Banana bags: IV fluid with vitamins, thiamine, and dextrose that is given to chronic alcoholics, which looks yellow from the vitamins.

Bat: BAT, blunt abdominal trauma.

Bite: A surgical stitch. "Take a bigger bite" means make the stitch longer.

Black cloud: Bad luck that a medical student or resident brings with him or her. (Example: "You've really got a **black cloud** on this service—we had fifteen admissions last night!")

Bleed them: Draw blood. (Example: "**Bleed him** tonight and check his PT and PTT.")

Blown: Dilated (pupil).

Blue bloater: Someone with COPD; particularly someone with chronic bronchitis who has trouble inhaling.

Bought the farm: Died.

Bounce back: Someone who was discharged who's readmitted.

Buff 'em up: To hydrate a patient and stabilize his or her electrolytes.

Campers: Kids with diseases for which there are special summer camps (cancer, diabetes).

Cheech: Give someone a patient with a bad problem. (Example: "The resident really **cheeched** me with that bleeder.")

Circling the drain: A patient who has taken a turn for the worse. (Example: "Better get some fluids in him, he's **circling**.")

City taxi: Abusers of paramedics and the free ride to the hospital.

CLDs: Controlled life-style doctors; doctors, like ER docs, who do not give continuity of care.

Code Brown: A bed full of excrement.

Crash and burn: A patient who is getting worse and needs to go to the ICU. (Example: "She's about to **crash and burn**.")

Crispy critter: A person burned to death.

Crump: Go downhill, die. (Example: "The patient with the MI **crumped** last night.")

CYA medicine: Cover-your-ass medicine (do extra tests and document everything), especially with a litigious patient.

Cystic: A kid with cystic fibrosis.

D&Ds: Death and doughnuts; another term for the M&M conferences because you always talk about patients who died and are served doughnuts.

Dead shovel: Guy who has a heart attack while shoveling snow.

DFO'd: Fainted, done fell out.

Dink: Fail to keep an appointment. Dink stands for DNK—Did Not Keep.

Donor cycles: Motorcycles (accident victims make good organ donors).

Down: Cardiac arrest (down time).

Drop a tube: To put, for instance, a tube down someone's nose and esophagus into their stomach.

Dump: A bad, hard-to-dispose-of patient sent by another doctor.

ETU: Eternal care unit (morgue).

Facinoma: A fascinating ER story.

Fertile Myrtle: A woman who gets pregnant repeatedly.

Flapper: Skin pulled off.

FLK: A funny-looking kid; a kid who comes in who doesn't look quite right.

FOS: In need of an enema, seen on X ray.

Gas 'em: Do an ABG.

Get burned: Make a mistake. (Example: "I really **got burned** when I sent home that guy with chest pain and he died.")

GGF: A workup on an old lady with a fever (granny's got a fever).

Glory ER: Exciting ER cases.

Go down the tubes: Get sicker.

GOK: God only knows.

Gomer: GOMER, get out of my emergency room—a patient you dread having.

Goober: Tumor—for example, on a chest X ray.

Gork: A patient on the way out; a hopeless case; brain dead.

GSW: Gunshot wound.

Hand them a Bible so they can study for the final: About to die.

HBD: Had been drinking.

Hit: An admission. (Example: "How many **hits** did you get?")

Hit hard: To get a lot of difficult patients in one shift.

Hurt me again: To get another train wreck after just working up one.

If you didn't chart it, it didn't happen: Variant of CYA medicine.

Incoming Scud: A train wreck coming by ambulance to the hospital.

Knife and Gun Club: An inner-city hospital that gets a lot of knife and gun wounds.

Larry Parker Syndrome: Someone who comes in after an accident complaining of pain, but who is really looking for an insurance settlement.

Let's get out of Dodge: Let's finish the case.

LGFD: Looks good from doorway. A patient who complains but looks fine.

Liver rounds: Friday afternoon social event for residents, attendings, and medical students where alcoholic beverages are served.

LOL: Little old lady.

M&Ms: Morbidity and mortality conferences where the ER doctors, residents, med students, pathologists, and other applicable specialists gather to discuss past cases in which there was error or the patient did not do as well as expected. Usually held once a week in the early morning; residents have to present the cases and are fair game for the audience of Monday morning quarterbacks.

Members: The abbreviation for mental retardation with cerebral palsy is MRCP, which also stands for Member of the Royal College of Physicians.

MUDPILES: Mnemonic device for anion gap: M(ethanol), U(remia), D(iabetic ketoacidosis), P(araldehyde), I(ron), L(actic acidosis), E(thanol), S(alicylate starvation).

Mutual of Sacrament: Medicare.

No code or **DNR (do not resuscitate):** No heroic measures.

Old trout: A patient who is old, but quick-witted.

O sign: Mouth gaping open when unconscious.

Perf: Perforate; to burst. (Example: "He had a **perfed** appendix"–appendicitis.)

PID shuffle: The walk of an obvious pelvic inflammatory diseased patient. The patient is young, female, holding abdomen, wide stance, hunched over, with a pronounced shuffle.

Pimp: Ask a medical student or resident difficult questions. (Example: "That surgeon **pimped** me on every artery in the whole damned gut!")

Pink puffer: Someone with emphysema who has difficulty exhaling.

Pit her: Give a pregnant woman pitocin to induce labor.

Preemie: A premature infant.

Pronounce: Pronounce dead.

Q sign: O sign plus tongue hanging out.

Road rash: Abrasions from a fall onto concrete.

Scoop and run: Grab you and go as fast as they can.

Scut work: Busy work—drawing blood, filling out lab slips, etc.

Seizer: A kid with epilepsy.

Send for labs: Draw blood, fill out the slip, and send the specimens out.

Send him redline: Send him directly and urgently.

Sickler: A kid with sickle-cell anemia.

Slammed: Variant of "hit hard," only worse.

Soldiers: Kids with chronic GI (gastrointestinal) diseases, like Crohn's disease.

Spark 'em: Defibrillate a patient.

Stat: Hurry up.

Stool magnet: A resident who always seems to get very sick, complicated patients.

Tank 'em up: To give a patient who is dehydrated a lot of fluid.

They're going to box like a smelt: Going to die.

Torture me: A variant of "Hurt me again."

Train wreck: A patient with multiple problems. (Example: "You wouldn't believe the **train wreck** I got—CHF, renal failure, and COPD.")

Treat and street: (Self-explanatory).

Turf: Send the patient to another service, such as transferring a patient on the medicine service to surgery. (Example: "I **turfed** her to surgery.")

Underdosing: An overdose that doesn't kill the patient.

Vitamin H: Haldol, a very powerful sedating agent for combative people.

WADAO: Weak and dizzy all over.

Walking time bomb: Someone with a disease that could be fatal at any moment, like an aortic aneurysm.

Wallet biopsy: Transfer.

Wheezer: An asthmatic.

WNL: Within normal limits; however, residents joke it means "we never looked." (Example: On a physical exam an ER doctor writes "abdominal **WNL**" and the resident says, "Abdomen, we never looked.")

ER: Yearbook

Sam Anderson
(Dr. Jack Kayson)

Abraham Benrubi
(Jerry Markovic)

Conni Marie Brazelton
(Conni Oligario)

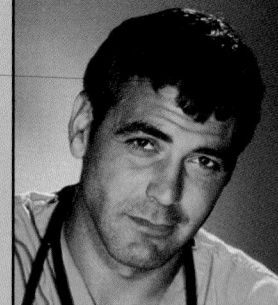

George Clooney
(Dr. Douglas Ross)

Ellen Crawford
(Lydia Wright)

Deezer D.
(Malik McGrath)

Anthony Edwards
(Dr. Mark Greene)

Ron Eldard
(Ray Shepherd)

Christine Elise
(Harper Tracy)

Tyra Ferrell
(Dr. Sarah Langworthy)

Yvette Freeman
(Haleh Adams)

Malgoscha Gebel
(Bogdanalivetsky "Bob" Romansky)

Carlos Gomez
(Raul Melendez)

Christine Harnoss
(Jennifer Greene)

Laura Innes
(Dr. Kerry Weaver)

Michael Ironside
(Dr. William "Wild Willy" Swift)

Eriq La Salle
(Dr. Peter Benton)

William Macy
(Dr. David
Morgenstern)

Julianna Margulies
(Carol Hathaway)

Lily Mariye
(Lily Jarvik)

Vanessa Marquez
(Wendy Goldman)

Glenn Plummer
(Timmy Rawlins)

CCH Pounder
(Dr. Angela Hicks)

Gloria Reuben
(Jeanie Boulet)

Rick Rossovich
(Dr. John "Tag"
Taglieri)

Sherry Stringfield
(Dr. Susan Lewis)

John Terry
(Dr. David "Div"
Cvetic)

Ming-Na Wen
(Deb Chen)

Kathleen Wilhoite
(Chloe Lewis)

Noah Wyle
(John Carter)

Lisa Zane
(Diane Leeds)

About the Author

Janine Pourroy is a senior writer at *Cinefex* magazine and the author of several movie tie-in books. She is a former public schoolteacher who developed Shakespeare for Young People programs at the elementary and middle school levels, where she continues to direct. She lives in Ventura, California, with her husband, Jim Hatch, and children, Jessie and Trevor.